BEYOND
THE BATTLE

BEYOND THE BATTLE
A History of the Land Dade Left Behind

Steven F. Rinck

Seminole Wars Foundation, Inc.
Dade City, Florida

Copyright ©2023 by Steven F. Rinck
All rights reserved.

Published by the Seminole Wars Foundation, Inc.
Dade City, FL
www.seminolewars.us

ISBN: 978-0-9821105-6-0

Front Cover Image: *Rays Through the Trees* by Kathleen Grau. Used with permission.

Frontispiece: Provided by the Author.

Back Cover Image: Current entrance to park, with banner announcing the park's Centennial in 2021. Provided by the Author.

For Nancy, who never fails to abide
my penchant for storytelling.

CONTENTS

Preface ix
Acknowledgements xi
Introduction xv

Chapter 1: THE DESTINY 1
Chapter 2: THE RECOVERY 9
Chapter 3: THE KOONCE SHOW 33
Chapter 4: THE SECOND DADE MASSACRE 61
Chapter 5: THE HARMONIOUS EXPANSION 87

Appendices:
A: Stories of Personal Experiences at the Park 103
B: The DADE MASSACRE and Dade Memorial Park 110
C: Dates of the Dade Annual Commemorative Events 127
D: Supervisors of the Dade Battlefield Property 129
E: Dade Battlefield Society Presidents 130

Image Credits 131
Endnotes 134
About the Author 146

PREFACE

I became a full time Florida resident during the summer prior to my senior year in high school. Originally from Pennsylvania where, from an early age, I had become immersed in and captivated by the richness of two hundred seventy years of American history. Becoming a Floridian immediately exposed me to four hundred years of a different history that had to be investigated, and I have been having a marvelous time doing so ever since. The requirements of education, jobs, marriage, and family allowed for only a reduced level of involvement in my avocational pursuits, but retirement laid it all at my feet once more.

My acquaintance with a fellow teacher and a rekindled friendship with a respected author and local history enthusiast led to a newfound passion for study of the Second Seminole War. Over the span of little more than a decade, I became involved with historical reenactments in Florida and Georgia, moved into leadership positions in both The Dade Battlefield Society and Seminole Wars Foundation, and was simultaneously student and teacher of the times when government and native people were in conflict over the Florida peninsula.

For close to one hundred forty years, the event that for so long had been called Dade's Massacre and the nearby City of Bushnell have been linked together. I discovered that the residents of that city and of southern Sumter County had developed a kinship to the battle site and had adopted that area as their own park long before the State of Florida did so officially. With a newly heightened curiosity, I volunteered alongside and interviewed dozens of local homeowners and businesspeople in an effort to better understand the strong bonds they felt for the now one hundred twenty acres that is Dade Battlefield Historic State Park. Their genuine acceptance of my company and their kind reception to my questions convinced me that the lesser-known story of a battlefield site post-conflict was just as fascinating, if not more so, than the story of the battle for which it is named. Both stories are, in essence, really just about the wonderful parade of people who were there and who are here, both before and during the fight, and especially now, Beyond The Battle.

Steven Rinck
Dade City, Florida
September, 2022

ACKNOWLEDGEMENTS

I have always loved to write. My mother, my teachers, and then a few (most were more circumspect with praise) of my university professors encouraged me to continue writing and supplied kind advice that helped me to hone the craft. Now, at this point in my life, I truly understand the importance of the advice, experience and wisdom of others that is making a difference in my current pursuits.

Thanks to Johanna Jones, a very active member of the Sumter County Historical Society, who more than once provided access to their files and records, for guiding me to sections pertinent to my needs. Patrick Swan, Seminole Wars Foundation life member, who steered me to the location of records and documents hidden within a morass of unsorted materials at our headquarters homestead. Fellow Foundation officers Debbie Harper and Rosa Sophia Godshall-Holden, for offering helpful tips on writing, publishing and marketing. My wife, Nancy Dorton Rinck, for courageously acting as the first reviewer of my draft manuscript, dutifully pointing out my errors as she read.

Present and former residents of Sumter County used their memories to provide interesting information that was not recorded elsewhere and, in some cases, to give access to photos that were. Thank you, Liz Sumner, Shanda Shaw, Dan McCormic, the Ed Force family, Karen Cloud and Bill Gruber. Special shout-outs to Karen for introducing me to meaningful interview subjects and to Bill for Park Service data and for regularly reminding me to get my work done since none of us are getting any younger.

Dade Park Services Specialist Kristin Wood shared the list of literally dozens of visitor programs that she oversees, and Robin Ringeisen, District Assistant to State Representative Randy Maggard, walked me through the process required to access State

Legislature records from 1845 to the present. Kathleen Grau generously volunteered the use, for the cover of this book, of her exquisite photograph of early morning sunlight shafts dancing with the oaks near the southwest corner of the park's replica breastwork structure. Copies of the Florida Historical Society's Herbert Drane correspondence collection were sent to me, unsolicited but nevertheless much appreciated, by fellow Seminole Wars Foundation board member Chris Kimball. My dear friends and prolific authors, John and Mary Lou Missall, for their encouragement, valuable advice on publishing and most especially for relieving me from much of the tedious tasks required to get my work into print. And the late Frank Laumer, my friend of forty-two years, for being so patient as I rifled through his copious records and for acting as my mentor in teaching by example how to use details in order to bring life to non-fiction reporting. My gratitude to all of you.

Two Sumter County officials were quite congenially helpful, and my sincere thanks to them both. Gloria Hayward, Clerk of the Circuit Court, graciously acted as a tour guide of the 1914 Courthouse and also gave me permission to photograph a painting of Judge Koonce hanging high on the wall behind the old courtroom bench, even recommending that I stand on that bench to get a better angle. And Mary Lovett, manager of the Office of the Sumter County Property Appraiser, located transactional records on the Dade land parcel and helped me to make sense of them.

One of my earliest research efforts centered on identifying and interviewing people having a variety of personal memories of their times at Dade Park. The reader will notice observations provided by them both in the body of this work and especially noted in the appendices. My appreciation is extended to the late Sam Coverston, Wayne Edwards, Frank Hamilton, Arthur Hayes, Gayle Hunt, Scrammy Hunt, Inez McMilland, Jean McNary, the late

Johnny Outlaw, Marsha Perkins, Steve Perkins, Ginger Bell Realmuto, Martin Steele, and Josephine Strong-Simmons.

And my long-overdue thanks to Mr. John Creedon, my junior high Civics and History teacher, who called a shy seventh grader to the front of the class, held up his report, "The Hidden Dangers of Foreign Aid," for all to see, and announced in his deep baritone voice, "This is the way that an excellent report is to be written." Talk about a confidence boost!

INTRODUCTION

A Florida newspaper article published in 1929 lamented that "Every school child has been taught the story of the Alamo…..and of the slaughter of Custer's cavalrymen….," but United States histories have drawn very little attention to Dade's Massacre, "the first daylight annihilation of American soldiers by Indians."[1] Yet today on that site, located one mile west of U.S. 301 on the south side of the city of Bushnell, Dade Battlefield Historic State Park's staff and volunteers do indeed honor the memory of the fallen through an annual reenactment and related ceremonies. They also commemorate a connection to a twentieth century conflict as well as provide facilities for themed community events, ranger-led nature activities, weddings, reunions, and family outings. The nature, character, and significance of this parcel of land, and of the people who have felt so connected to it, form the basis of the following true story.

Near Pemberton Ferry on the Withlacoochee River, six miles southwest of Dade Battlefield, ca. 1885.
Sumter County Preservation Society.

Chapter One
THE DESTINY

"Do you ever hear the screams of the dying men at night?"
Frank Laumer, 1978.

He had taken this route before, often enough, in fact, to enjoy a confidence in the journey that accompanies familiarity with one's surroundings. Ten years ago, he had led two companies of infantrymen north from Tampa Bay along this game trail and Indian path for the purpose of clearing, leveling, and straightening its course, while spending additional time on bridging its intersecting rivers. Care was taken to maintain a width of twenty feet for this improved thoroughfare, space enough for meeting the requirements of proper military traffic. And now, on the quite cool and rainy early winter morning of December 28, 1835, perhaps he even had a nostalgic thought of the times he had indulged his passion for racing Richard The Third, his fine-looking steed, along this Fort King Road. His next dismount, however, would be a tragic one,

Figure 1: Major Dade's Battleground.

the very last in the forty-two years of the life of Brevet Major Francis Langhorne Dade.[1]

Seven weeks after what was already being called Dade's Massacre, Major General Edmund Gaines led a command of 980 to the site, where they were met by a grisly scene of bodies and debris. Officers were identified, and theirs and soldiers' remains were buried with proper honors, including the performance of the Scottish dirge, "Scots Wha Hae" based upon the Robert Burns poem, "Bruce's Address to His Troops." As they played the funereal music the band members marched around the breastworks that had been hastily constructed by the last of the doomed. Six and one-half years later, all remains would be disinterred and reburied in Saint Augustine with other Seminole War dead under three coquina pyramids in the post cemetery of St. Francis Barracks, an area that is now the Saint Augustine National Cemetery.[2]

The Florida War, as it was known, had ended. The land of Dade Battlefield was scarred and seemingly devoid of humanity, and would essentially remain so for some time yet to come. Sixteen years prior, the Territorial Governor, William DuVal, stated, "No settlement can ever be made in this region, and there is no land worth cultivation." Mosquito County, covering an area today occupied by Sumter, Lake and Orange counties together with large portions to their south, had a census population of 73 in 1840. Reportedly there were so few that Joseph Sanchez, Marshall for the District of East Florida, certified, "That there are no inhabitants in the County of Mosquito except the military companies."[3]

Despite the fact that the Seminoles who were able to stay in the Florida Territory had sought refuge in the trackless Everglades, the Federal government was concerned that they might become sufficiently emboldened to try reoccupation of their former lands. As a mitigation effort, Congress passed the Armed Occupation Act of 1842, which offered one hundred sixty acres to any man who

Chapter 1: The Destiny

would live on the land he received for five years and agree to cultivate at least five of its acres. Importantly, he must also have been in possession of a functioning firearm and be willing to use it for protection against the Seminoles and their allies. In force for only nine months, the act encouraged over one thousand homestead applications in central and south Florida, including the land near Dade Battlefield. Even after the act's expiration, an older Congressional action offered public domain Florida land for only $1.25 per acre, and a newer one allowed American war veterans to make and receive even more public land claims. These opportunities proved to be very popular and ushered in a new wave of settlers to the Florida flatwoods, especially from Georgia and the Carolinas.[4]

The area near Dade Battlefield that would become Sumter County ten years hence did have a small number of hardy settlers by 1843, but was still relatively isolated from others in the region. Florida achieved statehood in 1845, and in January of 1853 the legislature took two actions: Establishing Sumter County on the 8th and on the 12th making it unlawful for any Indian to be present within the State.[5]

Named for the Revolutionary War General Thomas Sumter of South Carolina, the 900 square miles of this new county had an 1860 population of 1,429, many of whom having come from the General's home state. Some of the early settlers carried the family names of Beville, Bostick, and Anderson, with Collins being part of the second wave to come later in the century. In present-day Bushnell these names identify streets and avenues, and citizens carrying them have played roles in the evolving nature of the old field of battle.

Whereas the Bevilles were already well established and productive by 1857, most other newcomers arrived looking for fresh starts after their ways of life had changed dramatically in the post-Civil War South. Farmers Bostick and Anderson helped establish what would become Bushnell in 1870 by planting the area's first orange trees. By 1885 the grove was flourishing, and Bushnell was officially named in honor of the chief engineer of The Florida Railway and Navigation Company survey crew, John W. Bushnell, for his role in bringing a world of prosperity to town upon tracks carrying a ribbon of train cars. Citrus, cotton, corn, rice, sugar cane and all sorts of vegetables were shipped out, while supplies, mail order items and people shipped in.[6]

Then everything changed. A devastating freeze during the winter of 1894/95 caused orange trees to first lose their leaves and then, along with shade trees, trunks burst open with a force reminiscent of small dynamite explosions. Some grove owners replanted, most did not. Cattle ranching and vegetables, especially string beans, became the dominant economic activities.[7]

It was about this period that the Dade site fell into private hands and was passed among members of the same pioneer families for more than 35 years. In July of 1885, James W. Bostick traveled seventy-five miles on the Military Road extension to the United States General Land Office in Gainesville to remit $295.75 for a land patent of 119.50 acres in Sumter County. Receiving agent John Rollins noted that the property so reserved for purchase was the site of Dade's Massacre some fifty years previous. After returning home one week later, James made a warranty deed out to his cousin Luke Bostick and business associate Newton J. Anderson for the entire battleground, including the pond into which victorious Seminoles had sunk the six pounder cannon they had faced during the historic conflict. That deed was properly recorded, ironically ten months before President Grover Cleveland's signature was affixed to the grant that officially made James the owner, and two months, in fact, after James had died!

Not quite nine months would pass until Bostick conveyed full ownership to Anderson of the acreage that was destined to carry

Chapter 1: The Destiny

the legal description of what would represent the park to be named Dade for the first ninety-nine years of its State-owned existence. Over the following quarter century a growing number of spirited individuals would involve themselves in efforts designed to more permanently preserve the area for public use.[8]

The national shock and outrage that consumed Americans in the aftermath of Dade's Battle would eventually be displaced by reactions to the desperate Alamo struggle and the total defeat near the Little Big Horn River, but both established and newer residents of west central Florida kept the story alive. Politicians and others would remark about their youthful experiences there in wistful yet respectful terms.

Less than nine months after the loss of Dade's command, a call for a monument to be constructed at the ground of battle appeared in the Army and Navy Chronicle, a professional military journal. It would take another sixty-one years, however, before any actual congressional effort would occur.

U.S. Representative Stephen Sparkman of Tampa was born on a farm in neighboring Hernando County and had opportunities to visit the battleground during his youth. Serving in the House of Representatives for eleven terms, he introduced legislation in 1897 and numerous times thereafter that would have Congress provide, "for the marking and protection of the battlefield known as 'Dade's massacre' in Sumter County, Florida." Along the way, he sent a request to the War Department for

Figure 2: Stephen Sparkman.

all official documents relating to the Seminole wars that were of historical interest or value. By becoming better informed he hoped to become more persuasive, resulting in needed support for moving his bill out of the Committee on Military Affairs for a floor vote.

In his 1911 attempt, Sparkman retained wording that called for at least ten acres of land where a monument would be "erected upon the most sightly portion" of the battlefield, and required the War Department to preserve, protect and care for the site. That provision was not well received by Adjutant General B.P. McCain, and by 1915 Sparkman struck out such reference in H.R. 5771 in favor of verbiage directing that an outlay of $5,000 only be paid when a suitable site is provided that is "free of cost to the United States." In addition, the stated allocation would not be made until "a responsible legal association is created and pledged to care for whatever monument is erected under this act." Despite Sparkman's years of determined effort, none of these bills ever became law.[9]

Congressman Herbert Drane of Lakeland, in a 1930 letter to Colonel H.L. Landers, a lead officer assigned to the War Department's Historical Bureau, wrote that, "The burial trench, where most of the soldiers were buried, is still clearly indicated, never having been disturbed, and it was very clearly indicated during my boyhood more than forty years ago, when I often visited the place." An even earlier letter (1917) written to *Jacksonville Times Union* official B. Harrison found Drane depicting a time at which, "A number of the very old men of that day had the location of the incidents of the Dade massacre clearly fixed in their minds."[10]

A young lawyer who first learned the story of Dade while a North Carolina schoolboy, Sumterville resident James Koonce would occasionally walk around the property trying to visualize what had happened there in 1835. Destined to serve eight years in

Chapter 1: The Destiny

the Florida Legislature where during his final term he would offer a bill to purchase the site, as he walked and explored perhaps he thought of those trapped in horrific struggle in the way that a future historian would ponder by asking, "Do you ever hear the screams of the dying men at night?"[11]

The times were becoming favorable for a new destiny to ripen.

Archway Entrance to Dade Memorial Park, ca. 1954.
Courtesy of Dan McCormic.

Chapter Two
THE RECOVERY

"I have chosen a name for this hall, 'Tustenuggee Lodge'."
J.C.B. Koonce, 1924.

It is a presidential election year. President Theodore Roosevelt is advocating for Secretary of War William Howard Taft of Ohio to be his successor to run against the likely Democratic nominee, William Jennings Bryan of Indiana. The nation is in the midst of an economic growth period and is benefiting from increasing acceptance of its image as a world power. Americans continue their movements from farms to large urban areas, and immigrants steadily arrive at United States shores in more abundant numbers than ever before.

Ranking thirty-fourth out of forty-six in population, a pre-air-conditioned Florida had fewer residents than any other southern state. Signs of expansion and productivity in and beyond the surrounding counties had not yet been enjoyed by those living in the decidedly rural Sumter County of 1908. Its unincorporated community of Bushnell had no paved roads, running water or electricity, but there was a church, hotel and a few small businesses, as well as some optimistic talk of a chance to become the new county seat. And then there was this man, a resident of nearby Sumterville, who would quietly repair to a dense area of pine, oak and palmetto about a mile southwest of Bushnell, voluntarily trimming and clearing property that he did not even own. The man was an attorney, a three-term former state legislator, and a newspaper owner/editor, married with an eleven-year-old son, toiling away at physical labor whenever he could find breaks in his very busy schedule. The name by which most people knew this increasingly impatient activist was J.C.B. Koonce, and he had refused to be constrained any longer.

Figure 3: J.C.B. Koonce (1908).

So confident that it was only a matter of time before he and an ever-increasing legion of others who were so like-minded would eventually succeed in having a national park in their own backyard, "Why not," he must have thought, "take the lead in creating a more park-like atmosphere right now?" And although he would soon by universally acknowledged as being the spearhead of the effort, Koonce was not the first to yearn for such development.[1]

At the time of the storied battle, the land was described as a pine barren with abundant palmettos that provided cover for the Seminoles. By now, the pines were still predominant throughout Newton Anderson's eighty acres, but a number of beautiful oaks were providing a shady, pleasant environment in and around the location that marked the final hours of struggle in 1835. It was difficult to believe that all of them had appeared without human assistance.[2]

Koonce was not shy about using professional and political contacts to further his ambitions that were geared for the public good. Since purchasing the *Sumter County Times* in 1898, he had become quite skilled in the art of influence. When he so desired, his writing could be quite flowery and poetic, and he was personally

Chapter 2: The Recovery

known as an affable gentleman possessed of wit and humor. Beside his son Bernard, age eleven, others who believed in the potential of a park-to-be on what was as yet private property occasionally joined Koonce on his clearing and beautification project.[3]

On January 30, 1909, the Sumter County Courthouse in Sumterville was destroyed by fire. Most records prior to October 18, 1881 that had been stored there were lost. The following March third, ten years to the day that he bought it, James Koonce sold the Sumter County *Times* to Syd Graham, Sr. One week later, a syndicate of five investors from Washington, D.C., New York, and Philadelphia bought fifty thousand acres of Bushnell and its environs with the goal of selling residential lots to hundreds of families who would be new arrivals. Before four more years passed, the first bank in the area opened, Bushnell was chosen in a close election as Sumter's county seat, and eighty acres of the Dade site was acquired by a new owner. By 1913, Ralph Furman Collins was both president of Citizens Bank of Bushnell and mayor of the city, as well as already being the son-in-law of Mary Beville, the battleground purchaser.[4]

Figure 4: Breastworks site (1902). A man with horse and sulky stands on the east side.

And what of J.C.B. Koonce's physical labor and promotional efforts at what many were already calling "the park"? They not only continued, but increased in both frequency and diversity. A county judge for three years, he witnessed intermittent removal of pine trees going to sawmills, a business begun by the owner's father-in-law, Granville Beville, more than sixty years previously. The irregularity of this practice may be due, at least in part, to the frequent discoveries of musket and rifle balls so embedded in the tree trunks that they ruined saw blades and jammed machinery. In the process, however, the judge's land clearing efforts were being augmented.

Figure 5: Senator Duncan Upshaw Fletcher.

Associations for mutual benefit had always been important, and J.C.B. Koonce habitually sought after them. U.S. Senator Duncan Upshaw Fletcher, born in Sumter County, Georgia, began representing the people of Florida in 1909 and had just recently served on the Senate commerce subcommittee investigating the Titanic tragedy. When this former Florida House member was campaigning for reelection in the spring of 1914, Koonce, now a judge for four years, was at the ready. The two reacquainted themselves in Wildwood, from whence Koonce offered to personally drive the Senator through Coleman and Sumterville to a public appearance in Bushnell. As a pleased Fletcher later reported, "A big crowd welcomed me and when we went to the court house that night the place was packed." It's almost certain that the seventeen miles they traversed in Koonce's new 25 horsepower Ford touring car provided good opportunity for Dade Battlefield to be part of their conversation. [5]

Chapter 2: The Recovery

As previously mentioned, Herbert J. Drane had become familiar with the Dade Battleground as a young man. Now was the time to once again be in better contact with James Koonce, a colleague with whom he had served in the Florida House. Having succeeded Stephen Sparkman for what would become eighteen years representing Florida District One in the U.S. House of Representatives, he was moved to join in the call for the preservation of the Dade site. After assuming his new position in January of 1917, Drane found himself riding next to Koonce on board a train, very likely discussing their favorite topic of mutual interest. Soon thereafter he wrote to Benjamin Harrison of the *Jacksonville Times Union*, "I have introduced here in Congress a Bill looking to the proper marking by the Government of the battlefield known as Dade's Massacre." In May, the Florida House endorsed Drane's bill after having been informed that land had been secured for that purpose by The Ladies Civic League of Bushnell. Perhaps since war against the German Empire had been recently declared, the bill went nowhere. In response to a letter of appreciation from the Ladies Civic League for filing a new bill (without success) during the 1919 Congress, Drane inquired if that group's members could provide him any "local color" related to the Massacre's history. Clearly, he was already looking toward his third attempt for a bill planned for 1921.[6]

On the 28th of December, 1919, the 84th anniversary of Dade's Massacre, Gainesville lawyer and recent District Attorney for Northern Florida Frederick Cubberly visited the old place of battle. A prolific history writer and contributor to The Florida Historical Society Quarterly, he left for home sharing Koonce's view that steps to preserve the site must be brought to fruition.

Cubberly would go on to compose a fourteen-page booklet, "The Dade Massacre," that described not only that event but also the situations having led up to it and those that occurred following its conclusion. He used statements from battle survivors Private Ransom Clark and Halpatter-Tustenuggee, or Chief Alligator, in an effort to assure accuracy in reporting. Cubberly also did some editorializing by describing his personal site visit, terrain changes due to the passage of time and to human intervention, and the extent to which local citizens had gone in urging state and federal lawmakers to set the site aside for permanent recognition. He even included photographs of maps and other documents found within the Dade Monument at the United States Military Academy at West Point, New York, provided by its superintendent, Brigadier General Douglas MacArthur.

In a period of twenty-four hours spanning April 13 and 14, 1921, Representative J.C.B. Koonce and U.S. Senator Duncan U. Fletcher submitted "The Dade Massacre" to the Florida House and United States Senate, respectively, each body thereafter making it a part of their permanent records. Koonce had Cubberly's booklet printed at his own expense. Senate Resolution 40 ordered that it be replicated by the Government Printing Office in Washington and made available as a public document.

In the late evening of May 5, Koonce succeeded in having House Bill No. 183, his effort to establish Dade Memorial Park, moved up in the schedule for a final vote. His address was described the next day by a witness as "a masterly speech in defense of his bill, urging that there should be a unanimous vote for it. He pointed out that the death of these men was instrumental in gaining for the State a payment of two million dollars for the Seminole War claims from the United States." The bill passed 54 to 9. Florida Senator William J. Crosby of Marion County managed to steer a companion bill through the State Senate and the acquisition at last was approved. By May 11, the Legislature passed the bill that was then signed by the Governor eleven days later.

Chapter 2: The Recovery

It had provided two thousand dollars for the purchase of eighty acres from Ralph and Florence Collins and an additional three thousand dollars for improvements and surveying. Moreover, Senator Fletcher had assured Koonce and Crosby that if the State acquired the land, "the War Department would take over the place as a national monument and see to its care."[7]

Of course, J.C.B. Koonce's intention all along had been for the Dade site to be named as a national park. Less than one week after Senator Fletcher's assurance to that effect, Koonce received a letter from U.S. Representative Drane in which was stated since Congress was "holding down unnecessary appropriations on account of the financial condition of the Country, I have not yet been able to get a favorable report on the bill." Reportedly, the "financial condition" referenced remaining debt incurred because of the recent Great War. So as to maintain momentum, Koonce's attention had to remain with the State action that was already approved.[8]

On June 23, the Governor appointed three members to the Dade Memorial Park Commission that had been previously established by the Legislature. The commissioners were to receive no compensation beyond reimbursement for any personal expenditures made in the performance of their duties. They were Fred C. Cubberly of Gainesville, J.C.B. Koonce of Leesburg, and Alma Rowland, of Bushnell. Their charge was to provide "for

Figure 6: Frederick Cubberly, Alma Roland, J.C.B. Koonce (1922).

15

the enclosure and improvement of said tract of land and for the marking and appropriately designating the several points of historical interest within such park."

R.F. Collins for Eighty Acres of Land	*$2,000.00*
Surveying land and fixing boundaries	*15.00*
J.C. Allyn and Frank Cotton, contract for fencing park complete, erecting monument pedestal, building shed, small monuments to mark places where Dade, Frazier and Mudge fell, building concrete replica of breastworks, etc.	*2,200.00*
Frank Cotton building base for monument	*75.00*
Two Bronze Tablets for monument	*371.40*
Express on tablets	*14.82*
Bronze Soldier to surmount monument	*463.12*
Total	*$5,139.34*
Amount of Appropriation	*5,000.00*
Excess donated by the people of Sumter Cunty	*139.34*

In addition to this excess paid by people of Sumter County, they have donated sufficient funds to enable us to erect a stone archway at the entrance to the Park at a cost of about Six Hundred Dollars; to employ labor to clean up the grounds; to make other improvements --- and provide for a handsome stone bridge over the little brook which runs through the Park, --- as well as other improvements --- nearly One Thousand Dollars. [9]

According to the calendar, summer had just begun. Considering all of the paperwork still to be executed before final transfer of ownership could be realized, however, it would likely be well into the autumn season before all related items were actually finalized. But such mundane matters could in no way dampen the enthusiasm of the great number of Dade supporters, and a suitable

Chapter 2: The Recovery

celebration was already in the works. Although technically still held in private hands, Dade Memorial Park had its (first) dedication on Thursday, July 7, 1921. Despite the continual collection of storm clouds overhead, over four-hundred automobiles and almost one-hundred-fifty horse-drawn wagons filled with celebrants formed a steady procession all morning, ultimately bringing an estimated thirty-five-hundred people to the site. The dignitaries who had prepared speeches for the occasion were collectively wise in their support of the commissioners' decision to invite all those who braved the weather as well as the rough passage over winding, unimproved roads to begin enjoying the barbecue and basket dinners that awaited them.

Beginning the previous day, cooking pits were used to roast great numbers of beeves, goats, and hogs. Commissioner Roland was the director of the barbecue, as well as the distribution supervisor of all the fresh produce and baked goods that had been so willingly donated by a grateful citizenry. The local band played selections of lively patriotic music throughout the day, and there was a baseball game between teams from Bushnell and Inverness. One reveler observed that the day was for "consecrating hallowed ground in our own little front yard."

Commissioner Cubberly spoke of the history surrounding what had occurred here in 1835, and quoted heavily from his booklet that had recently been submitted to Congress.

Commissioner Koonce related how his long-held dream of creating this park came to pass due to the unwavering support of so many, and then shared a new dream with his listeners. The Judge challenged all citizens of Sumter County to join him in backing construction of a highway connecting Dade Memorial Park with Bushnell that would be dedicated to all those who had perished in the World War. Although he had no prior knowledge of it, this goal would be realized the following year through a county roadbuilding outlay of $136,000, $18,000 of which becoming the answer to the Judge's dream.

Mayor of Jacksonville and candidate for the Democratic nomination for Governor, John W. Martin, spoke of "Liberty, Life, and the Pursuit of Happiness." The final speaker, perhaps the most unique, was Sioux Chief Running Deer, sixty-one years of age, who was a witness to the Little Big Horn Battle of 1876. The son of Rain-In-The-Face, who claimed to have delivered the kill shot to Lieutenant Colonel Custer, Running Deer's tale added a Native American presence to the occasion.

At the end of the day, the band led those who were so interested into Bushnell for a static airplane exhibit. The pilot was unable to perform a promised flight demonstration due to mechanical trouble, but welcomed all to return Friday to witness that event. Those who did come back were also invited to attend the play, "Safety First," that would be staged at the Bushnell Opera House by the Bushnell Dramatic Club. By all reports, it was a standing room only performance. Money raised from ticket sales, along with donations offered by attendees at the previous day's ceremonies, were deposited for the benefit of the newly established memorial highway fund.

On September 21, the Florida Attorney General advised the State Comptroller that title to the Dade property was clear and a fee simple deed may be transferred from Ralph F. and Florence E. Collins to the State of Florida. The closing was completed on September 29, 1921.[10]

Weeks before the State had ownership, a collection of local volunteers were recruited by J.C.B. Koonce and became known as the Dade Massacre Association. This group was utterly dominated by the Commissioner. Although the senior partner in the Koonce and Hall Law Firm of Leesburg, he seemed to spend increasingly more time at the park. Professionals were hired to construct and

Chapter 2: The Recovery

install fencing and a building shed and, using native stone, to build a sixteen feet-high monument pedestal, with a few smaller monuments that marked spots where officers had fallen. Lloyd Ramsey and James Nairn chose those spots after having consulted a map drawn by a member of Major General Gaines' command in February of 1836, showing where the officers had laid. Nairn and others joined Koonce himself as he directed and participated in the construction of a concrete replica breastworks in a location in which small artifacts of military origin had been found. The original State allocation paid for these items plus two bronze tablets that were embedded on the east side of the monument pedestal and provided a brief description of the battle, listed names of all soldiers who were there, and proclaimed the grounds to be dedicated to their memory. Fully fifteen per cent of the funds were being spent on a bronze statue of a mid-nineteenth century soldier produced by a Salem, Ohio foundry, and destined to surmount the new monument pedestal.

Figure 7: Entrance Arch to Dade Battlefield Memorial Park (1922).

Beyond the Battle

Successful in receiving ample donations from the people of Sumter County, Koonce oversaw construction of a stone bandstand and the beginnings of a huge stone archway at the still unpaved park entrance. The Scotsman Nairn returned and was compensated for building the stone bridge spanning the drainage ditch north of the killing field site. Without authorization, he installed a cement plaque at the northeast corner that named the structure, "Auld Brig O' Doon" or, "Old Bridge Over the River Doon," the same as that of a fifteenth century stone bridge in Ayrshire, Scotland, that still stands today.

Figure 8: Cement plaque on stone bridge (2022).

Where once he had been a solitary laborer, the Judge now enjoyed the company of a small army of both paid workers and volunteers.[11]

A stated goal of the Dade Massacre Association was to have an annual picnic to commemorate the event that precipitated the longest Indian war in American history. Independence Day seemed to be the natural date, and with the laudable array of improvements made over the previous year, July 4, 1922 was selected for the formal park dedication. An estimated five thousand persons attended the event that was much more than a picnic, although once again Mrs. Roland made sure that free barbecue from twenty-five beeves and sheep was available, and a seventeen-piece band entertained throughout the day.

As before, notable public figures were in attendance, headed by Governor Cary Hardee. In his company were his Adjutant General C.P. Lovell, State Senator Wicker, Judge Charles Parkhill of Tampa, Commissioners Cubberly and Koonce, Mrs. Gertrude

Chapter 2: The Recovery

Darby, great niece of Major Dade, and Madeline Vaughn of nearby Center Hill, chosen Queen of Dade Memorial Park by a county-wide vote. Standing next to the Governor, Miss Vaughn pulled a cord to unveil the as yet soldierless monument, delivered a "beautiful address," and lastly pulled the silk cords revealing the bronze tablets. A heavy rain failed to diminish the spirits of either participants or onlookers.

Figure 9: Celebrants at 1922 celebration. Queen of Dade Memorial Park Madeline Vaughn is third from the left in the interior of the paper poppy-festooned Packard.

With supporters still determined to stir interest from the federal government, both President Harding and Secretary of War Weeks were invited but sent their regrets. Parkhill was the featured speaker, but Fred Cubberly captured the zeal of those there when he ceremoniously turned over the deed to Dade Memorial Park to Governor Hardee.[12]

As expected, an annual Fourth of July picnic continued in popularity even when unconnected to a large event. In their later years, lifelong residents of the area would speak of pleasant experiences at Dade Memorial from the perspective of the youngsters they were at the time.

Galye Hunt's father Enos was the first caretaker (1920-1925) hired by the Commission. Gayle talks of the large picnic every year from the 1920's through early 1940's and how, as a Boy Scout, he had helped with parking. His cousin "Scrammy" said that "Just about everybody in Sumter County gathered at Dade Battlefield. It was a big thing." Both of them remember a band in the bandstand, chicken pileau and barbeque. Retired teacher Sam Coverston, age 8 at the time, reported that although there were people everywhere, the ice cream, "a rarity in Bushnell in those days," was plentiful.

The late Burton Marsh, long-time Clerk of the Circuit Court, spoke fondly of the picnic and also of the prominent Florida and national leaders acting as speakers. A well-known attorney and former judge, P.B. Howell, Jr. wrote of long lines of tables covered with white butcher paper that supported mostly homemade platters of coleslaw, bread, and potato salad that accompanied the barbeque meats. Lunch was free but donations were strongly encouraged, and no one seemed to complain since there was never any park entry fee back then.

Beyond the annual picnic, succeeding months and years found people who would often stop by the park to see just what else J.C.B. Koonce had been up to. Having moved to Eustis after he became a judge in the Fifth Judicial Circuit Court in 1923, he would come to Sumter County weekly during slower docket periods to help local lawyers. He often held civil court proceedings at the park,

Figure 10: Native stone monument supporting the statue of a soldier in front of Tustenuggee Lodge (1940).

Chapter 2: The Recovery

perhaps at what twenty-first century culturists would refer to as his "happy place." By the time that Ike Hogan replaced Enos Hunt as caretaker in 1925, a host of new structures were there to be seen and enjoyed. The bronze soldier was now a silent sentinel atop the pedestal monument. A fifteen-foot-wide asphalt road, dedicated to soldiers of the World War, led to and through park grounds. A frame caretaker's residence was a few dozen yards to the soldier's north, and there was a year-old recreation building a few steps directly behind him to the west.

The Judge was known for emphasizing to citizens that it was not only Major Dade's command to be honored but also those who fought against them in order to defend their way of life. In a booklet he created as author, photographer, and publisher in time to be distributed during the centennial celebration of Dade Memorial Park, Koonce revealed to the reader eloquent evidence of his melancholy fascination for the plight of so many Native Americans:

> Many of these lilting Indian names still linger to give peculiar charm to our lakes and rivers. In these names one seems to hear the ripple of the streams and the music of the song bird. Sometimes they vision the forest primeval, the majestic oaks draped with the silver-grey moss, and sometimes, in twilights gloom apart, they suggest the pine trees whispering heart to heart. They bring thoughts of God's golden sunshine, the pallid silver of the moon, and the rainbow's glorious hues. They seem to bear the fragrance of the orange blossom, the wild jessamine and the modest violet, while not the least charm of all they speak the voice of freedom and liberty once the priceless heritage of the vanquished race.

Walled up to the windows with native stone, the 50' x 30' recreation building had an open-beam ceiling with exposed rafters, a cement floor, reception room, kitchen and serving room, and an impressive fireplace. On the occasion of the building's completion, Koonce said, "WE are the race with other customs and language," and "I have chosen as a name for this hall, 'Tustennuggee Lodge'." The Miccosukee word means "village war leader."

Figure 11: "Mick-e-no-pah, Chief of the Tribe" by George Catlin.

A replica of an original George Catlin painting was presented as a gift from Senator Duncan Fletcher. That work, prominently displayed in the lodge, was a portrait of Chief Micanopy, the Seminole leader who, by killing Brevet Major Francis Langhorne Dade, fired the opening shot of the Second Seminole War. [13]

During the Florida real estate boom of the mid-1920s, so many new arrivals poured into Sumter County that Dade Memorial Park became a temporary home to hundreds who pitched tents right on the property. The city council even gave permission for a tourist camp to be established there. [14]

With major structural components in place, Judge Koonce was earnest in his pursuit to create what he considered a family friendly, park-like appearance at this location of great historic significance. It seemed as if virtually every public park in the south that had even the slightest connection with military activity sported one or more old cannons with which people posed for photographs and upon which children climbed, so of course Dade had to have its own, too. Alma Roland helped expedite the receipt of a shipment of two Spanish American War-era Gatling guns that were located through

Chapter 2: The Recovery

the auspices of Representative Drane's office. Koonce wrote to Drane seeking further assistance, this time in procuring "plants and ornamental trees to make a real park," stating that he himself had planted over one hundred trees and many other plants just recently. Drane asked for a copy of the Cubberly booklet to help explain the need to the Chief of the Plant Industry Bureau of the Agriculture Department. Both the Congressman and the Judge were still pushing for a federal takeover of the Dade site.

Koonce used his creativity as he strove to, as he wrote, "have something to offer the Federal Government, and perhaps we will get Government help." Beginning to appear at Dade Memorial were concrete statues of soldiers and Indians, handmade and hand-painted by Koonce, that were peppered all through the woods. Some of these, though, had connections to the park that were not always clear. A pelican-topped fountain at least was dedicated to the memory of Captain George Washington Gardiner, military field commander during Dade's battle, but there were other structures that can only be explained as further solidifying the provincial nature of the park. Among these were a reclining Western Plains Indian with his arm propping up his head, a full-size alligator, and several free-standing small arches that were placed on the nicely-mown grounds.

Figure 12: Old Spanish Trail (1926).

One of the arches sported, at its zenith, a sign reading, "Pine Island," that for some unspoken reason became a popular spot under which couples would strike photographic poses. Another somewhat more appropriate favorite was a full-size, colorfully painted rendition of Osceola with a face that Koonce had fashioned by using a copy of the long-gone leader's actual death mask.[15]

When monies from the initial 1921 legislative allocation had been expended, the State did respond, from time to time, to calls for small amounts of additional funding. Further development and maintenance needs, however, still largely fell upon the citizens of Bushnell and Sumter County to provide. Despite near collapse of the New York Stock Exchange and the resulting Great Depression, an April 8, 1935, letter to Florida House Speaker W.B. Bishop found Commissioners Koonce and Roland reminding Tallahassee that it had been six years since last requesting assistance and that they were now in serious need of help. Yes, it was true that the Federal Emergency Recovery Administration (FERA) had approved a sum of nine thousand dollars for Dade, but that such national relief effort was limited only to labor with no provision for materials or supplies.

For months, Judge Koonce had been making the speaker's circuit of service clubs, social organizations, and commercial radio stations where he made the case for continued park support. What did the trick for him was to link the potential of a new revenue stream with a large, widely advertised battle centennial commemoration to be scheduled for December 28, 1935. By mid-May of that year, both of Florida's legislative branches passed resolutions of support for "suitable (centennial) ceremonies commensurate with the importance (of Dade's Massacre) in Florida history." It should be noted, however, that no appropriations for carrying out this resolution were delineated. Instead, the State Agriculture Commissioner was authorized to use any spare funds in his care for the celebration and its related activities.

There was additional language pointing to the expectation of large sums of federal money which would assist Dade Commission

Chapter 2: The Recovery

aims in coming to pass. It seems that Judge Koonce and Governor David Sholtz had been in contact with the office of Interior Secretary Harold Ickes about the possibility of a peace treaty being signed by a delegation of Seminole people who would be invited as the centennial celebration's honored guests. His department would, in such a scenario, be adding financial support to that which was ongoing from FERA. In fact, it was reported that Secretary Ickes was especially interested in such an endeavor since recently failing in a similar attempt at peace talks at West Palm Beach.[16]

Section 1 of the House/Senate Resolution authorized the Governor to appoint a Centennial Commission of the Dade Massacre which was to consist of eleven members. That number ultimately became Governor Sholtz, ex-officio chair; Judge Koonce, executive chair; Senator Truman G. Futch of Leesburg; Representative Samuel W. Getzen of Bushnell; Senator Fred L. Touchton of Dade City; Representative George F. Westbrook of Clermont; Mrs. Alma Roland of Bushnell, Treasurer of the Dade Memorial Park Commission; J.M. Lee, State Comptroller; Nathan Mayo, Commissioner of Agriculture; Representative John S. Burks, Dade City; and Senator Wallace Tervin of Bradenton. The first seven on this list would become present at the event they had helped to plan.[17]

At exactly one hundred years, to the second, that the few remaining soldiers were desperately trying to stay alive, J.C.B. Koonce officially opened the centennial observation of what was best known as Dade's Massacre at 10:00 a.m., December 28, 1935. A huge crowd was already present, with more still arriving on a chilly morning not too dissimilar to that of a century ago. Before another hour passed, more than five thousand people from all parts of Florida would be there.

While the Judge told of the Indian policies of 1835 which led to war, other public servants attended to the duty of maintaining order and safety. Sheriff W.T. Coleman handled parking and crowd control. Bushnell Utilities Superintendent Herbert Center arranged for acquisition and barbecuing of meats. Lunches were sold by the women of the Sumter County Health Council. Indian Agent W. Stanley Hanson supervised the nine (not the forty that Koonce had expected) Seminoles from south Florida. Adjutant General Vivian Collins of Saint Augustine commanded Florida National Guard members who were there. There was a host of other volunteers from a local population grown accustomed to taking care of their community park.

Figure 13: Centennial celebrants (Dec. 28, 1935). L to R: State Rep. George Westbrook (Clermont), State Rep. Samuel Getzen (Bushnell), Mrs. Ezell of Leesburg, State Sen. Fred Touchton (Dade City), Mrs. A.M. Roland, Treasurer of Dade Memorial Park Commission, a lady visiting from Kentucky, Judge J.C.B. Koonce (Tavares/Eustis), Secretary of Dade Memorial Park Commission.

Chapter 2: The Recovery

After stirring those present with his charismatic oral delivery, Koonce introduced Governor David Sholtz, a native New Yorker and personal friend of President Franklin D. Roosevelt. Sholtz, in a vibrant address, called for his audience to not forget the difficulties of the Florida pioneers who made it easier to enjoy the comforts of the present day. Nodding to current events, he also warned of attempts by Communists to introduce false doctrines into our country. He termed the day's festivities as a rededication to ideals rather than a celebration of war.

Figure 14: Centennial Dignitaries. L to R: First Row: Representatives of Seminole Tribe and Indian Agent W. Stanley Hanson. Second Row: State Rep. Samuel Getzen, State Sen. Truman Futch (Leesburg), Gov. David Sholtz, Florida National Guard Adjutant General Vivian Collins (St. Augustine), Judge J.C.B. Koonce, State Sen. Fred Touchton, State Rep. George Westbrook.

Following the Governor were other notables, including Charlie Billie, a Seminole guest, who stated, "We have come a long way to help you to have a big time today. We want to be friends."

At about noon members of the Daughters of the American Revolution and the United Daughters of the Confederacy placed wreaths at the soldier monument while patriotic airs were played by the Ocala High School Band. A roll call of the men of Dade's command was read, followed by the playing of Taps, then a twenty-one-gun salute at the log fort performed by the National Guard.

Music was almost continuously played in the afternoon, with the Ocala group being joined by the American Legion Auxiliary Band out of Lakeland. Along the way, Judge Koonce introduced additional speakers while public officeholders and other dignitaries mingled with the visitors. A special broadcast by WRUF in Gainesville originated onsite. The Seminoles, three men, four women, and two babies had not reenacted anything nor had any treaty been signed. They did, however, actively participate in what perhaps was the first public living history exhibition on the grounds. Camped, as it were, outside a museum building where items under glass could be viewed, the Seminole guests were cooking in a pot suspended over a fire done in the traditional four-log style, explaining what they were doing to interested visitors. At the end of the day and as the crowd thinned, car headlights were turned on to assist in a safe cleanup and departure activity. The Seminoles simply boarded the Tamiami Trailways bus in which they came and rode off into the night with Agent Hanson. And no one, not Koonce, not any legislator, not even Sholtz himself, was heard to make mention of the fact that only six months before, the Governor officially pronounced establishment of The Florida Park Service, an action that would affect significant and long-lasting change for Dade Memorial Park.[18]

Tablet placed near the gazebo in Dade Memorial Park after Koonce's death.
Photo by the Author.

Chapter Three
THE KOONCE SHOW

"Because They Love Him."
Dedication plaque at the entrance of Dade Memorial Park, 1922.

In 2008, the author became a volunteer at Dade Park and began making regular appearances there, a practice he continues to the present day. He discovered, as countless other visitors had, two bronze tablets permanently affixed in stone that are in praise of J.C.B. Koonce. The one at the front gate pronounces Koonce as the person who made the original structure at that location possible; the other one, installed near the park's gazebo, is in memory of the gentleman following his death in 1948. Together they speak of a person who was a sturdy, imaginative and earnest leader who was loved by the people of Sumter County. This observer accepted the idea that the subject of such praise must have made significant contributions to the park, but then-current matters discouraged further investigation. Four years later, curiosity caught up with industry and a decade of research on this man of esteem was initiated. For someone so well associated with Dade Park, Koonce only lived a little over three years in Bushnell and resided in many places in a tri-county area including Sumterville, Ocala, Eustis, Tavares and Leesburg. Bushnell folks, however, mostly considered him one of their own. This chapter serves as a biographical sketch of Koonce and also of other personages of note who had influence on the development of Dade Battlefield Historic State Park.

Figure 15: Portrait of J.C.B. Koonce by Domini, Courtroom of 1914 Sumter Courthouse.

JAMES COUNCIL BRYAN KOONCE
1870-1948
Secretary of The Dade Park Memorial Commission

Anyone who is well-informed of the post-Second Seminole War history of Dade Battlefield will surely agree that its greatest champion was J.C.B. Koonce. As reported by Belle Hamilton, Secretary of the Lake County Chamber of Commerce, "Too much credit cannot be accorded Judge Koonce for the work he has done in bringing the park to its present status, often by the arduous labor of his own hands."[1]

Although there would later be two half-siblings more than twenty years his junior, little James was the only child of Calvin Luther Koonce, a Confederate Army veteran, and Nancy Ann

Chapter 3: The Koonce Show

Nunn. The most recent addition to a large number of Koonce relatives scattered throughout Lenoir (his birthplace), Jones, and Craven Counties, North Carolina, his lineage tracked back five generations before reaching an ancestor who was birthed in a place other than one of those locations, namely George Michael Koonce, Sr., born 1704 in Baden-Wurttemberg, Germany. At that time, the family surname had been Cunitz.[2]

By the time the United States of America was established, Koonce family members embraced their new nation with so much zeal as to name new babies after famous achievers. Some examples and their birth years are as follows:

Christopher Columbus Koonce	1778 and 1833
Thomas Jefferson Koonce	1845
George Washington Koonce	1853 and 1873
Andrew Jackson Koonce	1870
Woodrow Wilson Koonce	1912
James Monroe Koonce	1916

The Koonce family of antebellum southeastern North Carolina showed interest in civic service in a big way. An 1857 meeting of the American and Whig Party appointed James' Great Uncle Emanuel F.B. Koonce as Secretary, then three more of the same last name as convention delegates. In 1880 Jones County Democrats nominated a Koonce for Sheriff, another for Deed Registrar, and yet a third for Delegate. All three were unanimously elected. His sizeable extended family played a major role in influencing James to seek a career in public service.[3]

At age 10 James stated a preference to be known as J.C.B. Koonce and was already developing leadership skills. According to a local newspaper reporter present at the year-closing assembly at Kinsey's School in LaGrange, "Master Jimmie is an orator for one of his age, and in a clear and self-possessed manner he extended a hearty welcome to the audience."

Two years later, then a student at LaGrange Institute, "Master J.C.B. Koonce" was presented with a medal for elocution. He had also developed an interest in Seminole Indian history, particularly what was then called "The Dade Massacre" of more than one hundred United States soldiers by Seminoles numbering up to one hundred eighty strong.

That summer, J.C.B. and his father journeyed to Florida, leaving his mother back home. Finding shelter in Sumterville, they began working in citrus groves and did a little merchandising, as well. Another two years had passed when he returned to LaGrange to live with his mother and enroll in Kinston College, graduating four years later. Soon thereafter, his mother died and Koonce again made his way to Sumterville where he took a teaching position while also finding time to study law under Colonel J.C. Langley of Leesburg. By 1891 he was admitted to the Florida Bar and became Langley's junior associate.

Shortly after beginning his law career, J.C.B. met Frances "Fannie" A. Howse and embarked on what would be an exclusive four-year courtship that culminated with a marriage in 1895. The newlyweds thereafter made their first home together in Gainesville, as that was the location of J.C.B.'s new practice, in partnership with Syd L. Carter, a state attorney.

Described as a "young gentleman of brains and irreproachable character," Koonce's most obvious attributes were perhaps his drive and ambition. One year after his son Oliver Bernard ("O.B.") arrived in 1898, Koonce purchased the *Sumter County Times* from Walter Graham and won election to what would become three consecutive two-year terms of representation in the Florida House. So, before the age of 29, J.C.B. was simultaneously a successful attorney of growing renown, both editor and publisher of a weekly

Chapter 3: The Koonce Show

newspaper situated in the seat of Sumter County, and now a lawmaker representing that same county in the Tallahassee Legislature. Editorially characterizing himself as, "a 'tar-heel' by birth, but a Sumter County Cracker by adoption," his circles of influence continued to widen and increase in number.[4]

During the final two years of one century and the first four of the next, J.C.B. Koonce served on a variety of legislative committees, including Constitutional Amendments, Public Printing, State Pensions, Temperance, and Judiciary, which he chaired during the 1903 session. He championed the proper care of hogs, sheep, goats, beeves and even bats, while strengthening the punishment for carrying concealed weapons. He made the case for funding summer schools (failed) and offered a bill making incurable insanity grounds for divorce (approved). He convinced the Legislature to declare the community of Wildwood a legally incorporated town and railed successfully against a proposed Constitutional amendment dealing with the election of Circuit Judges. "I am opposed," he said, "to the continued changing and mutilation of our Constitution, and to every change which necessity does not demand. I fail to see the necessity for this change; it has not been demanded either by the people or the conditions of our State affairs."

It should be noted that during his six years of legislative service, Representative Koonce had never proposed that the State should acquire the Dade's Battle property, preferring instead in joining others seeking federal recognition of that lionized location.[5]

As his final term was fading in the spring of 1904, Koonce attended a Jacksonville meeting of the supporters of newspaper magnate and New York Congressman William Randolph Hearst, who had expressed interest in becoming the Democratic nominee for President. J.C.B. placed his own name into consideration as an at-large Florida convention elector who would be pledged to Hearst. Many of his fellow newspaper editors in central Florida wrote glowing endorsements of him in their own publications. "Well known and popular" (*Tampa Times*); "...stands high in the councils of the Democratic Party" (*Gainesville Sun*); "We know of no better qualified man in the State" (*Dunnellon Advocate*). One uniquely strange recommendation was received from *The Southern Advocate* of Brooksville, but most likely appealed to Koonce's sense of humor. It read, "He claims to be a newspaper man, but we don't know how that is, as we never see his paper. We suppose it is too small to be allowed to wander so far away from home." That statement was followed by the advice, "We say vote for Koonce early and often." That July in St. Louis, within sight of the World's Fair, Koonce's man lost to another New Yorker, Alton B. Parker, with total votes 679 to 181. [6]

In 1909, Attorney Koonce sold the Sumter County *Times* to Syd N. Graham, brother of Walter Graham from whom he had purchased it eleven years before. On February 25, 1910, another former *Times* owner, Sumter County Judge John A. Tillman, succumbed to tuberculosis, a disease with which he had been suffering for years. Relatives and close friends (including Koonce) had been expecting his demise for several weeks. The Governor appointed J.C.B. to complete Tillman's unexpired term, and he was formally elected in his own right, unopposed, to the position in May. He moved his law office from Ocala to Sumterville, where he rented a house for himself and son Bernard. His wife Frances remained in Ocala with her mother, adult siblings and their children. [7]

Koonce would continue moving both his business and residential addresses over the next twenty years, as his requirements changed. It was in this period that his site work and personal lobbying of Central Florida Congressional officials kept the preservation and developmental needs of Dade Battlefield at the forefront of his thinking. But he did not neglect his family either, often traveling back-and-forth between Sumterville and Ocala (by 1914,

Chapter 3: The Koonce Show

between Bushnell and Ocala) to spend time with Frances. Frequent campaign trips were many times accompanied by Bernard, but on the night of June 22, 1915, Koonce found himself alone after his Ford struck a log and became inoperable. He was forced to complete his journey to Ocala on foot for seven miles.

During the summer of 1918, J.C.B. Koonce felt the need to participate in the war effort by providing service to members of the American Expeditionary Force who still remained in Europe. With Bernard in the naval reserves in Charleston, Koonce resigned his county judgeship and applied for a position with the National War Work Council of the Young Men's Christian Association (YMCA). He passed the physical examination for overseas work and applied for a passport three days before the war-ending armistice was signed. He was five feet five inches tall, had nearsighted blue eyes, dark brown hair, a fair complexion and had attained the age of forty-eight years.[8]

The January 1919 trans-Atlantic crossing took thirteen days, thankfully in the absence of German submarines. Koonce spent a day sightseeing in Winchester, made his way across the English Channel, after which a train took him and the other YMCA workers to Paris. While there he noticed the stark difference in appearance between the gloriously beautiful Versailles Palace and the rest of the city that was still seemingly wrapped in wartime precautions against destruction. One more journey of one hundred sixty-five miles brought Koonce to Chaumont, where he was placed in charge of a "hut."

A hut was a large, spacious wooden building serving as the center of social life for military personnel. It took the place of an American home, church, school, club and stage. All huts came with tables, chairs, benches, musical instruments, games, stoves and kitchen equipment, some of which came from the United States with most found by purchasing agents scouring England, Spain and Switzerland. The "Y" acted as a post exchange, too, selling cigarettes, candy and other personal items. Library assistance and religious services were also provided. Koonce was one of four hundred sixty-two attorneys among the more than eleven thousand YMCA workers in Europe, whose main goal was to improve and maintain the morale of American soldiers.[9]

Figure 16: A YMCA "Hut" in France (1918).

J.C.B. Koonce made it home in August, returning to Bushnell where he opened a law office and became a boarder of Hattie Eddins and her three adult children. His wife and son were still residing in Ocala. One year later, he declared his intention to once again run for the State House, representing Sumter County, and won handily in November, 1920. Prior to taking his seat for the 1921 legislative session, he moved his residence and law practice to Leesburg in Lake County.

During the first week of session in Tallahassee, J.C.B. offered three bills specific to Sumter.

Chapter 3: The Koonce Show

HB 181: To authorize the Sumter Board of County Commissioners to build and maintain roads in Sumter County by contract.

HB 182: To authorize the Town of Center Hill to fix license and occupational fees.

HB 183: To establish the Dade Memorial Park in Sumter County, Florida; to provide for a Commission to acquire the necessary land, to define the duties of such Commission, and to make an appropriation to meet the expenses of acquiring and establishing such Memorial Park.

One month later, House Bill 183 and its companion in the Florida Senate were approved by both House and Senate vote, and signed by Governor Cary Hardee on May 2, 1921.[10]

The reader has already been made aware of the joyful 1921 celebration that lauded the State of Florida's action to preserve the Dade site, as well as the more formal 1922 dedication of the park. Still incomplete at that July 4th dedication, in September the magnificent stone entrance arch was virtually finished when the plaque honoring Koonce pictured in Figure 17 was permanently installed on its west side.

Figure 17: Plaque affixed to the entry arch to Dade Battlefield Historic State Park.

Beyond the Battle

The Secretary of the Sumter County Chamber of Commerce, Clarence E. Woods, reflected on the touching sentiment displayed, writing "May he as well as his posterity…derive from this graceful deed of a grateful people the virtuous satisfaction flowing from the unusual ante-mortem eulogy (and) by his devoted acts and countless hours given in rain and sunshine, has…reclaimed from possible oblivion the sacred spot where fell Dade and his men, and made of it a shrine from henceforth for all who truly love the Land of the Free and the Home of the Brave." [11]

On June 12, 1923, the Governor named J.C.B. Koonce as Judge of the newly created Fifth Judicial Circuit Court of Florida that included both Sumter and Lake Counties. He bought the J.S. McCauley bungalow on South Ninth Street in Leesburg so that Frances, Bernard and he could finally have their own home. Already a popular public figure, over the next several months Koonce found himself being honored and celebrated by hosts of his fellow citizens throughout the Fifth Circuit and beyond.

Professionally, he would be elected and serve in the same post for the rest of his life, most often running without opposition. The types of cases he adjudicated varied greatly, including divorce, banking scandal, voting irregularities, manslaughter, gambling, foreclosure, and the disqualification hearing of another judge. In 1930 he presided over the murder trial of Former Hernando County Sheriff W.D. Cobb. Successive governors borrowed Koonce from his Lake/Sumter District to fill in for absentee jurists in locations all over central Florida, coast-to-coast, such as Clearwater, Bradenton, Titusville, Ocala, Daytona and Orlando.

The Judge's off-duty schedule was quite busy, as well. He continued to perform physical labor in the park when he could, nurturing the battlefield and keeping it neat. He remained the primary person emphasizing the importance of having Dade Park present itself as half-recreational and half-memorial mecca for visitors,

Chapter 3: The Koonce Show

even into his seventies. The owner of Barnes Restaurant on Main Street, Blondell Barnes, remarked that Koonce would regularly come in for breakfast "with moss on his head and shoulders" after working on the battlefield. He was also greatly sought after as a speaker in a number of different venues, including The Florida Bar Association, Federation of Women's Clubs, Junior Chambers of Commerce, Daughters of the American Revolution, the Silver Springs Attraction, and numerous Rotary Clubs. He was a member of the Eustis Rotary Club for twenty-three years with perfect attendance (having moved to a house on Morningside Drive in that city in 1927), club President from 1937 to 1938, and was a valued member of Knights of Pythias, Knights Templar, Scottish Rite Masons, and Shrine. [12]

While collecting testimonials on the qualities of J.C.B. Koonce's nature, the author consistently found examples of his helpfulness, generosity and genuine interest taken in the lives and activities of others. Wildwood resident Maud B. McCall, a student at Florida State University in 1923, gave her "full appreciation" to the Judge for providing her with "materials and ideas" for a college essay. Lifelong Bushnell resident Gayle Hunt admired that Koonce "took care of the park like it was his living room." In 1998, a Leesburg attorney who knew J.C.B. very well, wrote, "…he was always most kind and considerate to all," and that "…one couldn't help but love and respect Judge Koonce."

The man himself, a frequent recipient of praise and honors, retained a sense of humility laced with humor that served him well when making more serious points. Addressing an audience of Rotarians in 1940, he took no credit as an after-dinner speaker but referenced his "clients now reposing in Raiford State Prison" as classifying him as an unentertaining "after-trial speaker whose words were too short with sentences too long." Going further, he remarked, "it is unfortunate that many persons take our courts as a joke, but anyone who has sat upon the bench knows it is no joking matter." Ten years earlier he had said, "The legal profession …gives such real and important service to the public…and no other profession is faced so continually with strong temptations, nor are those temptations anywhere also so consistently resisted."[13]

Perhaps the single portion of his character most representative of Koonce's spirit was his hobby of spending nights and weekends creating statues of human and animal figures. It was not about decorating the grounds of Dade Memorial Park, as least not at first. His interest in craftsmanship could be traced back to this North Carolina boyhood when he took up carpentry and construction of utilitarian objects made out of wood. Years later, when the day of State acquisition of the Dade site drew near, he began fashioning plaster figures and installing them on park grounds. Others found their way into his court chambers at Tavares, festooned by the early 1930's with renditions of animals and Native Americans. When occasions warranted, he would remove his creations to donate for charitable causes or to simply give as gifts, as he did at Christmas time in 1932 when each fellow Rotarian received either a dog or monkey. Never did he sell or otherwise financially profit from his pastime.

Later experimentation led to Koonce's development of a gummy rubber composition of his own making which, after coupled with a hardening furnace constructed by his son Bernard, led to the creation of hundreds of colorfully-painted dogs and other small animals that were almost indestructible. Their distribution time each year coincided with Easter, the place being the grounds of the Sumterville Methodist Church. Every child coming to the yard, regardless of church affiliation, went home with a new toy friend. Later in the day, the Judge made his way to his other hobby, Dade Memorial Park, to conduct an Easter egg hunt where his rabbits, squirrels and chicks went to all children under ten years of age.

And why Easter? Because it represents all that is new, hopeful and good. "Besides," he said, "it seems to make the children happy, and nothing is more delightful to me than a happy child." [14]

A widower for nine years, James Council Bryan Koonce died at the Lake County Medical Center in Eustis on September 15, 1948 of a heart attack following a long illness. Funeral services were held on the 17th at St. Thomas Episcopal Church of Eustis, with its pastor Reverend A.L. Burgreen officiating and Methodist Church of Adamsville Reverend C.C. Martin assisting. Six active pallbearers were all attorneys or jurists as well as personal friends, coming from Bushnell, Tavares, Ocala, Eustis and Leesburg. All members of the bar and bench of the Fifth Circuit were honorary pallbearers as the Judge was laid to rest in Adamsville Cemetery. Survivors were his son O.B. Koonce, half-brother Claude Koonce, half-sister Alice Revels, niece Patsy and nephew William. The "father" of Dade Battlefield Historic State Park was 78. [15]

Figure 18: U.S. Representative Herbert Jackson Drane (1929).

HERBERT JACKSON DRANE
1863-1947
Supporter of The Dade Park Memorial Commission

Herbert Drane was born in Simpson County, Kentucky, and attended schools there until he attained fourteen years of age, at which time continuing illness forced him to quit. Four years later he moved to Macon County, Georgia for employment in the lumber industry, but once again failing health changed his destiny. Following his doctor's advice to move as far south as the railroad would go, he arrived in Kissimmee, Florida, in 1883.

H.M. Drane, Herbert's cousin, helped him to get a job as an employee of the H.B. Plant South Florida Railroad, at that time working in Polk County on a line going to Tampa. In a few months, Drane was managing work crews and became one of the first residents of the newly-founded town of Lakeland. He was instrumental in establishing a permanent depot there, around which the new town expanded rapidly.

Chapter 3: The Koonce Show

Discovering his talent for entrepreneurship as railroad work went on west, Drane started the area's first drugstore, and for a while became editor of the *Lakeland Cracker* newspaper.

Finding the time to bring his Kentucky bride, Mary Wright, back to their new home in Florida, by the age of 25 Drane began a four-year term as mayor that was followed by service as a Polk County commissioner. In between, he purchased an orange grove and started an insurance business, later being invited to advise the State on the development of uniform forms of state insurance.

During the first two decades of the twentieth century, Drane represented Polk County in both the State Legislature and Florida Senate. Just before the United States entered into World War One, he began a U.S. Congressional career that lasted until 1933. He thereafter served on the Federal Power Commission, returning in 1937 to private life and his pursuits in real estate, insurance, property management and citrus farming.[16]

Both business and government service provided opportunities for Drane to explore special personal interests. Included in his Florida District 1 representation was the community of Tarpon Springs, and he very much enjoyed working with Greek-American interests in protecting the sponging industry. He was really enthusiastic on the subject and had his Washington office filled with sponges of all sizes. Once he had intervened with the U.S. Immigration Service to expedite approval of the entry of a Greek Orthodox priest being detained at Ellis Island. For that and other reasons, the shining new sponging boat that had been proudly referenced as "the aristocrat of the sponge fleet" was christened *The Herbert J. Drane*.

A first for a congressman was experienced when he was invited by Seminoles to accompany them for a conference at an undisclosed wilderness location. In the spring of 1931, members of the Everglades, Cow Creek and Big Cypress groups came to Drane's

Lakeland residence to invite him on a three-day trip on what today could be called a fact-finding mission. The following November, a two-truck convoy driven by Richard Osceola and Johnny Cypress transported the representative and two associates to a pre-established camp, returning him after two nights spent there. It is uncertain if any subsequent report dealing with discussion topics was ever made. [17]

Drane was well-known for his willingness to engage in conversation about Florida history. Shortly after Florida House and Senate bills to purchase Dade's battleground were approved, he continued to press for federal efforts that would complement the result of that action. When he casually mused about how the United States government should contribute war relics for the purpose of decorating the site of the Dade massacre, other nearby Congressional members were heard to say, "That's a new one on me," "I had read upon every important battle but don't remember any such name," and "You must be mixed up in your information and mean the Alamo massacre in Texas." Drane also left evidence by many letters in which he made cases for official Federal recognition of important historic sites, especially those connected with the Seminole wars. He regularly made Dade Battleground first on the lists of Second and Third Seminole War sites in letters sent to a variety of officials. In a March, 1930 letter he received from The Florida Historical Society, President Arthur T. Williams stated, "I see in this morning's *Times-Union* that you had gotten the War Department to mark battle fields, forts, etc., in Florida, and am writing to congratulate you on good work and interest in a matter of so much historical value. It is a fine thing that you have done and will be greatly appreciated by all who are interested in the preservation of historical spots." [18]

Being aware of his interest, J.C.B. Koonce found it convenient to request Representative Drane to act as a conduit between what

Chapter 3: The Koonce Show

he perceived as Dade Memorial Park's requirements and attempts to procure facility support from the national government when state government was reluctant to provide it. In a letter he had typed himself and for which he apologized for numerous errors, Koonce thanked Drane for securing Florida Governor Doyle Carlton's opinion in favor of a federal takeover of the Dade site. He then went on to detail the park's current needs that included a "gasoline tractor mowing machine," the caretaker's back pay, and one hundred concrete benches. While not making any assurances, Drane offered respect for the Judge and his positions. "I know of no public service which has been rendered in Florida which has been more unselfish or more beautiful than the service you have rendered in that connection." He continued by writing, "For that reason and for the further reason of my long-time affection for you, I would under no circumstances do anything in connection therewith which did not meet your approval." [19]

In July of 1946, Drane was on vacation in Waynesville, North Carolina when he stumbled and fell on an uneven spot in a sidewalk, thus fracturing his hip. By then a widower for five months, Herbert Jackson Drane would remain confined to his bed for the remainder of his life until its end came on August 11, 1947. He was an Episcopalian and member of a host of civic and social organizations, and was the recipient of the honorary degree of Doctor of Laws from Florida Southern College. [20]

Figure 19: Alma Roland holding a child (1931).

ALMA ELIZABETH WISE ROLAND
1884-1969
Treasurer of The Dade Park Memorial Commission

Alma Wise, eldest child of John and Eugenia (Colllins) Wise, was born in Lake City, Florida. Her family lived on a Columbia County farm, and she was expected to take on a good share of responsibilities early on in helping to manage two sisters and two brothers. By all accounts she was a good student and the first in her family to receive a high school diploma.

At age 24 she married Allen Malone Roland, a public school teacher in Gainesville, Florida. By 1920 the couple were living in Bushnell with their five-year-old son Kyle, and baby girl Muryl. Allen was then an attorney, an occupation he maintained for the rest of his life.

The Rolands were actively involved in both professional and social life in Bushnell, with Alma eventually becoming president of the Woman's Club, and Allen, being well regarded by his fellow lawyers, including J.C.B. Koonce. Alma excelled in leadership roles in the community and developed a reputation as a take-charge person. Her organizational skills were surely a factor in her being appointed by Governor Hardee as one of the three commissioners, along with Koonce and lawyer Frederick Cubberly of Gainesville, of the Dade Memorial Park Commission in 1921.

As with the customary manner of address at the time, Mrs. A.M. Roland displayed good stewardship over not only the commission's financial records, but also the management of events at Dade Park, both large and small. She took the lead in acquiring two Spanish-American War-era Gatling guns for display near the battlefield's concrete breastworks. Alma was reappointed by a succession of Florida governors over twenty-eight years, up to the 1949 disbanding of the Commission. A widow for two years, Alma Elizabeth Roland died in Bushnell on January 3, 1969.[21]

Figure 20: Frederick Cubberly.

FREDERICK C. CUBBERLY
1869-1932
Chairman of The Dade Park Memorial Commission

A case could be brought to one's attention that Fred Cubberly's first publication, the thirteen-page essay, "The Dade Massacre," comes in second to the decades-long efforts of J.C.B. Koonce as a valuable contribution to the preservation of what is today Dade Battlefield Historic State Park. It was, in the author's opinion, the climactic tool that was so skillfully utilized by Koonce to reach that long-sought goal.

Less than a year after Frederick Cubberly was born in Chillicothe, Missouri, his family moved back to Marion, Indiana, where his father George had earlier begun his Civil War service as a first lieutenant in Indiana's 17th Infantry Regiment. Fred completed his sophomore year of high school before moving to 160 acres, three miles from Archer, Florida. Since there was no high school in that area, the sixteen-year-old took up surveying and civil engineering work and became a phosphate mining superintendent in his early

Chapter 3: The Koonce Show

twenties. In like manner as J.C.B. Koonce, Cubberly did not attend law school, but in his case used a correspondence school to study the subject and was admitted to the Florida Bar at the age of 29 in 1898.

A bachelor who had just opened a law practice in Bronson, he boarded at the home of Dr. William and Sallie Hicks, sharing the dinner table with them, two teachers, and the treasurer of Levy County. His reputation rapidly advanced, and by 1903 he was a customs collector at Cedar Key, United States Court Commissioner for Levy County, a prominent attorney, and the husband of Mary Etta Hancock of Archer, the daughter of a well driller.

The Cubberlys, four in number as of 1910, purchased a home in Gainesville. Appointed as United States District Attorney for Northern Florida by President Taft, Fred lost that post under the new Wilson administration, but was appointed municipal court judge in 1914 and served in that capacity for the following two years. At the start of his new job, he secured passports for himself, Etta and their two young daughters. The stated purpose for needing the passports was "to go abroad temporarily and to return within two years." But they all remained home, at least for the next three years, and then things became weird. From his appointment as a notary public on June 8, 1917, up to his appearance at Dade Battlefield on December 28, 1919, there is no family or public record of Fred's activity or whereabouts. Perhaps coincidentally, or not, this time period coincided with the United States' entry into European war and its forces' return home. A notation in Jess Davis's *History of Gainesville* of 1966 reads, "During World War I, he (Cubberly) was not a member of the armed forces but served his country in many ways which were 'top secret' then and are best left so now." In later years, Etta Cubberly wrote, "We 'did our bit' at home."[22]

Beyond the Battle

President Harding returned Fred to the post of U.S. District Attorney for Northern Florida, one which he would retain until his death. His job kept him busy prosecuting violators of the Volstead Act of Prohibition, clamping down on the practice of peonage, a form of slavery, and various sources and levels of corruption. As with many federal attorneys, Cubberly was also the target of intimidation tactics, some allegedly originating with the Ku Klux Klan.

Now that daughters Hazel and Helen were completing high school, his job was steady and secure and the country was heading into a prosperous decade, Fred could give more attention to his favorite avocation, the study of history. The 1921 "The Dade Massacre" was his first significant publication, one in which he took much pride. And it did, indeed, finally rally legislative decision-makers to do the right thing by Dade Battlefield and pointed to him as a logical choice for chairman of the newly-formed Dade Memorial Commission.

The 1920's continued to witness a series of papers on Florida history that were penned by Cubberly. His 1922 "Andrew Jackson, Judge" appeared in *The American Law Review*. It documented court cases conducted by the future president while he was military governor over the new Territory of Florida. And Fred was not averse to submitting his pieces to literary magazines. The March 1924 issue of Herbert Felkel's *Sunshine Magazine* offered pieces on baseball, fake publicity artists, poetry, "The Making of a Gentleman," and the Cubberly offering, "The Siege of Camp Izard."

While first a member, later officer (Vice President (1927), President (1932)) of the Florida Historical Society, he published in the Florida Historical Quarterly essays on a Florida/Georgia boundary dispute (1924), John Quincy Adams' role in the Adams/Onis Agreement by which the United States acquired Florida (1926), the history of Fort King (1927), and the history of Pensacola's Fort George (1928).

Chapter 3: The Koonce Show

Breaking away from work and writing was a rarity, but Fred did make time in 1926 to take Etta and Helen to Cuba for the Christmas holiday, retuning to Key West on the SS *Northland*.

Although experiencing a paralytic stroke in 1930, he recovered enough to continue duties from his office. Frederick C. Cubberly, age 62, suffered another, very sudden, stroke on August 11, 1932, from which he did not survive.[23]

Figure 21: Ralph F. Collins.

RALPH FURMAN COLLINS
1883-1959
Conveyor of the Dade Battle Site to the State of Florida

History was of little concern to him. Dwelling in the past did not seem to be a worthy exercise, but achieving an understanding of present trends and opportunities could perhaps be useful in predicting future success. Ralph Collins seemed ready to try anything that had good potential for profit.

The son of a Georgia farmer and grandson of a Confederate soldier, Ralph followed his father, William Allen Collins, to Florida in 1899 at the age of sixteen. The two eschewed traditional agriculture in favor of draining pine resin for turpentine production. In addition to the naval stores business, William also started a general store on Main Street in Bushnell and wished to use that as a starter enterprise for Ralph. Calling it the R.F. Collins and Company sent that message publicly.

By the time he was twenty, Ralph Collins was being touted as "Bushnell's young merchant prince," and was engaged to Florence Elizabeth Beville, two years his junior and a member of one of the

Chapter 3: The Koonce Show

earliest pioneer families in the area. They made a handsome couple and began their 1904 marriage in a very secure manner.[24]

By the time he was thirty, Ralph Collins had carved out a corner in the back of the store being run by his father and turned that spot into the town's first savings bank. He acted as cashier for the Citizens Bank of Bushnell, operated a fire and casualty insurance company, and began the initial of what would become more than five years serving as Bushnell's first mayor. While occupied with these diverse duties, Collins secured a state charter for the bank, served as chair of the Liberty Loan Campaigns during the Great War, and was appointed a notary public by Governor Napoleon Broward.[25]

Figure 22: Beville Family at Bushnell railroad crossing. Florence Beville in wagon with white hat (ca. 1895).

Ralph's wife played a significant role in his continued success, and he used her family's connections to further not only his own ambitions but also to encourage development of the city and its surrounding county lands. Even before the official 1853 creation of Sumter County, Florence's grandfather, Granville Beville, Jr., brought his young family from Georgia and settled in an area between present-day Sumterville and Coleman. He grew cotton and operated the first water-powered grist mill in the area. "Beville Mill" was quite popular since it could grind corn, run a cotton gin, and even saw lumber. Much of the profits were used to acquire more land, a practice that resulted in ensuring Granville's descendants remained in prominent positions within their communities.

Ralph Collins seemed to have it all. A clever entrepreneur with a strong work ethic, his wealth and influence were well enhanced through association with the Beville family. In 1917, already on his way to becoming one of the largest landowners in the county, Mayor Collins bought, from his mother-in-law Mary Culbreath Beville, the eighty acres that included Dade's 1835 field of battle. Three years later he granted timber leases for turpentine production on that tract to the Fussell family, who quickly assigned some of them to a third party, the Peninsular Naval Stores Corporation of Jacksonville. When he learned that the legislature had finally agreed to preserve the property through purchase, Collins managed to secure quitclaim deeds from all lessors just one day before he and Florence sold the Dade site to the State of Florida for two thousand dollars, just twenty-five dollars per acre. That was the equivalent of four hundred dollars per acre as of the time of this writing.[26]

During the first half of the 1920's, Citizens Bank continued to prosper under Ralph's leadership. In October of 1922, a modern, two-story building opened on the south side of Bushnell Plaza between North Market Street and, perhaps fittingly, North Beville Street. As had many other businesses, the bank benefitted from increased capitalization opportunities that had become prevalent during the Florida land boom. Less than four years later, the boom turned into a bust. Real estate values fell dramatically, and there were panic-driven bank runs by uninsured depositors all through Georgia and Florida in July of 1926, including one on Citizens

Chapter 3: The Koonce Show

Bank of Bushnell. Collins locked the doors and was actually seen by witnesses to be running the three blocks from the bank to his home at 114 West Noble Avenue with a wheelbarrow full of cash! The bank was soon permanently closed, and he bore the brunt of blame for people's financial losses. Bushnell would be devoid of local banking services for the next twenty years.

Shortly after the panic debacle, Ralph still resided in Bushnell but was working as both the secretary and the treasurer of Acme Title Company in Eustis. Now, the father of four children at home in 1930, he reported to census takers that he was the operator of a small farm.

Figure 23: Citizens Bank, Bushnell.

He managed a store in 1935, and by 1940 was employed as a stenographer at a construction business. During his final years, Collins served as the clerk for the Sumter County Selective Service Board.

He remained involved with his community and, along with Florence, saw to it that their children were well educated and prepared for their adult lives. Despite his public prominence, most acquaintances found him to be a humble man in private life.

After a long illness, Ralph Furman Collins died in Leesburg Hospital at the age of seventy-five years.[27]

Park Rangers (l to r) Glynn C. Edwards and Paul McAllister flanking soldier statue, 1964.
Glenda Mitchell Family

Chapter Four
THE SECOND DADE MASSACRE

"This is a battle site, not a Bushnell park."
Frank Laumer, 1979.

The commemoration of the Dade Battle Centennial had been, by every measure, a resounding success. The event drew many new people to the park while allowing those who already enjoyed familiarity with it to remain justifiably proud. And, to be sure, the picnics, family celebrations and other recreational activities there continued, especially since the free admission was most welcome by a population not yet fully recovered from financial hard times.

The Dade Memorial Park commissioners, working with elected representatives and other officials, continued to issue reasonable requests for money from Tallahassee. All too often, however, encouraging news of a good funding bill would be ultimately pared down to a significantly lesser allocation. In 1937, a Florida House bill appropriating $10,000.00 made it out of the Senate at $3,750.00 and was signed by the governor for $1,985.00. In 1939, what was a hopeful $7,500.00 in May was finally realized in August as $3,100.00. In between these two efforts, there was one year during which absolutely no funds flowed from the State Capitol. Park Superintendent Ike Hogans' 1938 salary was covered by the citizens of Bushnell, but a modest request of $1,000.00 for maintenance was rebuffed by the State cabinet. A secretary did send a note, however, saying, "We are sympathetic, but we can do nothing about it now because we do not have the money."

When European war drums began beating, economic jitters made cost savings and conservation the norm across the nation. Whereas the budget for furnishing and maintenance of the governor's mansion was cut by ten percent and the Confederate pension fund by fourteen percent, Dade Memorial Park was walloped with a fifty-three percent reduction. And yet, throughout the four post-centennial years, the Bevilles and other families held annual reunions at the park and the Fourth of July continued to draw from three to four thousand celebrants every time.[1]

Section 4 of the original statute by which the State acquired Dade Battlefield stated that the property would be turned over to the United States War Department for future care as soon as the park was designated as a National Monument. Congress never approved such an action, and the Federal Government declined assumption of ownership, so operational control and maintenance of the site passed by default to the City of Bushnell until such time as the State could take over.[2]

Although the War Department never accepted the park's transfer, there was a time during which it "borrowed" the property and controlled all access in and out of the grounds. During World War II, three units of the Army Air Corps were located outside, but close to, the city of Bushnell. About 1,530 acres to the northeast of town were leased for construction of two airfields by the 841st Aviation Engineers Battalion from Jacksonville, and beginning in 1943 pilots and air crews were being trained there. Construction of "Bushnell Army Air Field" was assisted by personnel from the 91st Army Air Service Group, 73rd Bomb Wing out of Leesburg. A portion of the airfield was also used by the Dugway Proving Ground Mobile Chemical Warfare Service Unit to support experimentation with mustard gas, phosgene, and hydrogen cyanide in the semitropical environment of the Withlacoochee State Forest.

Chapter 4: The Second Dade Massacre

When America entered World War II, Park Superintendent Vernon Huff and his wife Delma were living at the park. They had chickens, cows and hogs, the last of which enjoyed slop that was collected from the Army camp that had developed there. In early 1943 Huff moved to Mount Dora and recommended that his brother-in-law, Edwin Jessie Woodard, take over his job. Shortly after they had moved in, Ed and his wife Nell were informed that all civilian personnel had to vacate the park due to wartime security concerns. Once again, the Dade property's appearance and function were changed, not by altering or removing what was there, but by adding numerous temporary buildings in such a way as to collectively transform the grounds into an actual military base. Archival records housed at today's park contain an original sketch of the Army encampment that shows the soldier statue, Tustenuggee Lodge, bridges, breastworks and statuary, surrounding and

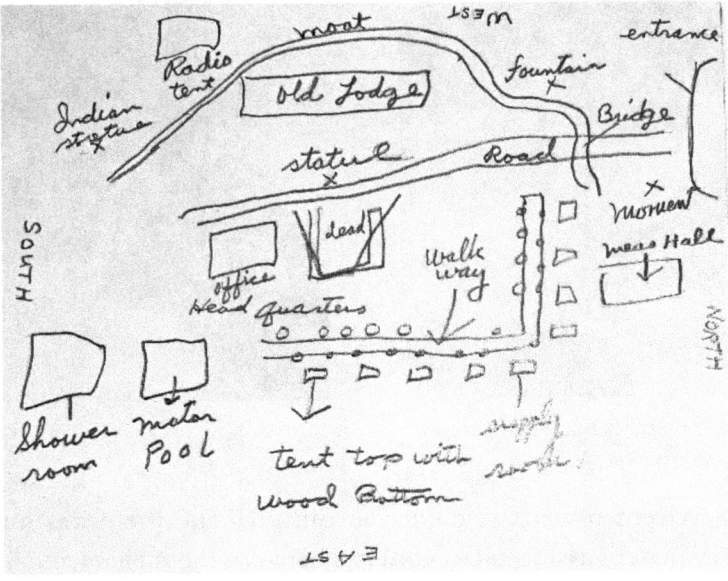

Figure 24: Sketch of WWII Army camp at Dade Park (1944).

surrounded by a headquarters, mess hall, supply building, shower room, radio shack, motor pool, and multiple residence tents.

A part of these same archives are thirteen photographs taken by and of Ed Force, a soldier who was stationed there at the time. For the most part, they show the soldiers at ease at a variety of locations around the park. Although it's likely that the intention was to document their experiences, there would be another wonderful benefit for later researchers. Behind the subjects are visual records of not only the military base, but also of statues and stonework from the early park days that today no longer exist. There is even an image of a young woman standing next to the well-defined, full-size rendition of Osceola that Judge Koonce had so carefully created.

Figure 26: Ed Force near supply room and a barracks hut (1944).

Figure 25: Three uniform styles (1944).

Servicemen were welcomed in Bushnell and there was much mutual benefit as a result of contacts between the military and local citizens. Dade Memorial Park, along with some private property beyond its borders, had begun its transformation into an Army

Chapter 4: The Second Dade Massacre

camp as early as 1942. Although it was hard to accept the park being a closed Federal site, those manning the American home front were becoming accustomed to rationing and doing without in the spirit of wartime sacrifice. Civic and church groups led the way in organizing social and religious activities for young G.I.s. Furniture was donated for their recreational use in Tustenuggee Lodge and weekly USO dances were organized in town. Junior Woman's Club members encouraged all women to show their patriotism by doing "everything possible for the welfare and entertainment of our boys."

Figure 27: Karl Stevie at park entrance (1943).

Figure 28: Soldier and Evelyn Allen with Koonce-made Indian.

While a proud supporter of the war effort, Koonce remained steadfast in his insistence that Dade Memorial Park be reopened to the Bushnell community. Aside from civilians missing picnics and other forms of recreation, the park's lodge was the only building that provided a fairly large interior space on the south side of

Sumter County, meaning that for the previous twenty years it had been used for meetings and other events with great frequency. The Judge met with Army officers in local command positions for the better part of a year before they finally agreed to reopen a portion of the park just in time for the Fourth of July celebrations of 1943. In an article published in the Sumter County *Times*, the Judge wrote that citizens "will be allowed to visit Dade Park…and enjoy the north portion of the park, holding picnics, etc., until midnight." The public was restricted from areas south of the drainage ditch, however, and at day's end the entire park and was once again off-limits to unauthorized personnel for another year.[3]

Figure 29: Young woman with Osceola statue made by J.C.B. Koonce (1943).

Newly activated in January of 1944, the 622nd Signal Aircraft Warning Company provided training in the operation and maintenance of aircraft warning equipment, including the development of new tactics and techniques. Dade Memorial Park provided housing for all the servicemen from the 622nd, as well as a significant number of personnel from the other units who had already been stationed there, from January to June of 1944. In her research paper, "Bushnell During World War II," Madeline Carr states, "Forty officers and 434 enlisted men of the 622nd Signal Air Company were assigned to train in a technology that was the best-kept secret of World War II." The secret was radar.[4]

At war's end the remaining vestiges of the Army's presence were removed and the park reverted to full access public use.

Chapter 4: The Second Dade Massacre

Found to be either missing or damaged, however, were many of J.C.B. Koonce's paintings and Indian relics that he had generously donated to continue his decades-long mission to improve the park. At almost the same time, though, his spirits were uplifted when he learned of the success of his efforts in lobbying U.S. Senator Claude Pepper of Florida to introduce a bill authorizing the federal government to build a replica of the monument to Dade's command that occupied a prominent position at the U.S. Military Academy at West Point, New York. The process required to turn a Senate bill into a reality was filled with hurdles, including the need for a companion House bill and approval by the War Department, and the Judge was relieved when President Harry Truman signed the act into law on June 19, 1948. All that had to be accomplished to create and install the replica was for the Florida Legislature to bear the expenses of the project. Koonce had recently been reappointed to the Dade Memorial Park Commission, and with his established contacts at the State Capitol he knew it could get done. Sadly, he passed away less than three months after the signing, at a time when the legislature was not in session, and though approved, the new monument was never created.

Figure 30: Edwin and Lynell Woodard.

In 1949 the legislature dissolved the Dade Memorial Commission and moved Dade Park under the auspices of the Florida Board of Parks, naming members of a new advisory board that would communicate local needs and desires. It became clear that such desires were aimed toward returning to the recreational park of pre-war memory. Improved picnic areas and a barbecue pit ranked highly, as well as facilities for baseball, tennis and shuffleboard.

For over five years now, Edwin and Nell Woodard were living back in the 24' x 30' frame house north of Tustenuggee Lodge and on the south side of the drainage ditch. The house already existed prior to the State of Florida's purchase of the property in 1921, although electricity, running water and indoor plumbing came much later. Ed was so laid back that he occasionally shot squirrels from his front porch and summoned his dogs, Hitler and Tojo, to retrieve the quarry that eventually became part of some fresh stew for picnics under the trees. Recalling those times decades later, his niece would describe her experiences at the park as a "dream place (and) time to grow up in."[5]

Figure 31: *Newly completed lodge building (1956).*

By 1955 both the advisory board and the Woodards were gone and the Florida Park Service had finally taken firm control of Dade Park. Full-time State management was tolerated by the local community, since the promise of favored improvements were being realized. A reliable patron of the park appeared in the presence of State Representative (later Senator) James Culbreath ("J.C.") Getzen, Jr. Having been raised in Sumter County and succeeding his older brother Samuel into both of those offices, J.C. Getzen successfully shepherded legislation through that appropriated $21,285 in 1953 for a new lodge building, rest room and barbecue shelter, and $39,000 in 1955 for a concrete block ranger's residence, garage with storage, and a museum/office building to replace Tustenuggee Lodge. Funding for better roads and various

Chapter 4: The Second Dade Massacre

pieces of equipment was expended, along with improvements to water and sanitary facilities. About the same time that the 1920's superintendent's residence was torn down, a children's playground appeared in 1959, and Getzen managed to squeeze out another $8,000 for two new picnic pavilions in 1961. Bushnell's newspaper, The *Sumter County Times,* published an article that seemed to reflect a renewed sense of civic pride when describing the fireproof barbecue pit as "one of the finest in the state," and the illuminated double tennis courts as being "rated the best in any park in Florida." The rate at which such positive developments were being made without losing the site's natural beauty was dazzling, and local residents were witnessing what benefits were possible when the State was finally paying the attention that had seemed to have been missing for so long.[6]

Still, time, use, and Florida weather continued to effect other kinds of change. Large parts of Judge Koonce's Dade Park were vanishing. The soldier base and ornate entry arch, both fashioned out of stone and mortar, were crumbling and had to be taken down. Also showing signs of wear, the pelican, Indians and small arches were disappearing. The concrete cannon replicas marking

Figure 32: Visitors in Dade Battlefield Museum (1976).

where officers had fallen were removed but soon reappeared at the hands of unknown persons.

A case could be made that the most significant change was the establishment of the small museum onsite; not since, at $28,000, it was the single most expensive structure, but rather because it symbolized a movement on the part of the Board of Parks to emphasize the historic aspect of the property as much as its recreational value. It was true, as Superintendent Arthur Clark reported at his retirement, that the number of visitors steadily increased from 1956 to 1961, sometimes to as many as five to six thousand per month. Their purposes to come most often were tied to picnics, parties and reunions, but those also venturing into the museum learned, perhaps for the first time, the reason why the State of Florida preserved and named the property as it did.

Figure 33: Silent combat symbols, Dade Battlefield Museum (2022).

At the museum's dedication on July 4, 1957, Dr. Kathryn Abbey Hanna of Winter Park, Chair of the Florida Board of Parks and Public Memorials, spoke of plans to build museums in every historically significant state park in Florida. "Parks in these locations," she said, "should mean more to the people than just places for them to visit for picnics and recreation." Dr. Arnold B. Grobman, Director of the Florida State Museum, agreed but characterized the Dade museum as a monument to a "fusion of education and recreation which I would like to see extended widely throughout Florida" rather than one that just memorializes war. Among the approximately one hundred dedication audience members, it seems unlikely that any

Chapter 4: The Second Dade Massacre

one of them would have been anticipating the emotion-filled controversies that lay ahead.[7]

The Second Seminole War, at six years, seven and one-half months, was the longest war in the first 196 years of American history. For Dade Battlefield Historic State Park, controversies over how it should be operated and the manner in which it is presented to the public lasted eight times longer. In a position paper written in September of 1985, Jon W. Dodrill, former District 5 Biologist for the Florida Department of Natural Resources made an effort to express his frustration, explain his position, and offer an example of how compromise could mitigate controversy. Here is what he wrote:

> I do not believe in pitting north against south, native against nonnative, young against old, or state government against local people. I feel no joy when I read newspaper articles intended to do just that. There is too little love, respect, and exchange of knowledge in the world today to spend time fueling the flames of mistrust and prejudice which people have tried so hard to extinguish. The staff at Dade Battlefield and myself want to continue to work on good relations with the people of Bushnell and Sumter County. We also want to do our best to interpret as accurately as possible the events which took place here and the items and artifacts remaining on the property to all who visit here. This is our job. We want to keep lines of communication open with historic society members and community leaders. I respect those who take the time to state their feelings and opinions regardless of whether they disagree with mine. That means at least we're talking and communicating.

Beyond the Battle

The controversies of which Dodrill wrote were some of the same that troubled his friend Frank Laumer, a real estate developer who, twenty-three years previously, had developed an avid interest in Dade's Battle and the larger war in which it became the opening act. Laumer had written the award-winning "Massacre!" a book that described events before, during and after the battle in such detail as never had been done before. Dodrill's letter inspired him to compose his own one month later in which he supported his friend's position to Park Superintendent Lieutenant Wayne Edwards. Citing his over two decades of research and investigation, Laumer stressed "that effective steps be taken as soon as possible to correct well-intentioned errors of the past. Above all I believe that the park should be dedicated and maintained first and foremost as a battleground and only second as a playground." He followed up with proof that the concrete breastworks replica was inaccurate in size, shape and position, a plea to allow grass and palmettos to overtake trimmed lawn, and recommended the Civil War soldier statue be removed and given, "with proper ceremony," to the people of Bushnell. [8]

Figure 34: Park visitors with Gatling gun at concrete breastworks with soldier outside museum in distance (1960).

Chapter 4: The Second Dade Massacre

CONTROVERSIES

Drainage From "Death Pond"

This one is not much of a controversy but more like a difference of interpretation. From time to time, water may be seen flowing under four stone bridges, three of them close together near the park's main entrance, the fourth appearing near the southern boundary line. Over the years, local citizens and visitors alike have made references to this long depression as a brook, stream, channel, and creek, while in reality it is really a drainage ditch. Webb's Pond, now on park property and sometimes referred to as "Death Pond" due to its role in Dade's Battle, originally was a spring-fed body that provided the ditch with continually flowing water. Sometime not long before State ownership, the flow was temporarily dammed and workers converted the ditch into a canal, since they lined its bed with well-fitting stone to help stave off erosion. As the water returned, so did an accompanying population of fish.

When the new lodge and visitor center were being constructed in the mid-1950's, nearby limestone mining operations plugged the spring, thereby permanently ending the flow. Rainfall is now the only source of any visible water in the canal.

The Park Entry Fee

Since coming under State ownership in 1921, there had never been an entry fee at Dade Park. Sixty-five years later, a carload of visitors was required to pay one dollar for the group. Opposition to this imposition was taken to the highest local form of government. On May 20, 1986, a new Sumter County Resolution formally called upon the State of Florida to remove the new fee, since Dade was "a place of public, historical significance and there should be no charge for admission to it."

Beyond the Battle

Almost exactly five years later, the Florida Park Service approved a new fee schedule of two dollars per vehicle. In an opinion piece published by the local newspaper, Park Manager Jeff Montgomery defended the charge by citing a poll in which voters indicated a preference for such a fee in lieu of dipping into general revenue dollars for the support of state parks.[9]

<u>The Cannon</u>

The 108 artillery and infantrymen on Dade's march were accompanied by a cannon and limber pulled by four horses along the Fort King Military Road. The U.S. Model 1819 six pounder, nicknamed "Walking Stick" because of its length, played an active role in the opening battle of the Second Seminole War, and a more unusual one when the fighting had ceased.

After the battle, the Seminoles and their Black allies disabled the cannon tube and dumped it into a pond just a short distance from the soldiers' bodies. Fifty-four days later, men in Edmund Gaines' command buried the human remains and placed the tube muzzle-down on the grave after having extracted it from the pond. Another six years passed before more soldiers arrived to exhume all remains and transport them to Saint Augustine for reinterment. In the reports, no mention was made of the cannon-turned-monument. What, then, happened to it? There are several theories, each having supporters:

1.a. Ingloriously removed for scrap during the Great Depression or a metal drive during World War II.

1.b. With thousands of potential witnesses, nobody ever reported such action.

2.a. Retrieved in 1842 and accompanied military remains to Saint Augustine and placed into the mass grave that had been prepared there.

Chapter 4: The Second Dade Massacre

2.b. Reports would surely have been made and also appeared as part of the vivid description of the ceremony in the Saint Augustine News.

3.a. Taken back north, as were some of the other artifacts.

3.b. This artifact weighed 750 pounds and would have needed a wagon or carriage for transportation in the pre-rail era.

4.a. Thrown back into the pond for a second time.

4.b. A 1976 search of Webb's Pond performed by the Florida Archaeological Society found cannonballs and smaller items. A private search with state-of-the-art equipment performed in 1998 found nothing.

5.a. After the exhumations, rolled back into the large depression and covered with mounds of dirt still containing buttons, buckles, coins and lead shot.

5.b. Only a deeper archaeological excavation could confirm.[10]

The Fence

Today there is a walk-in gate on the south side of Dade Battlefield Historic State Park to accommodate the rare occasion of a pedestrian seeking entry. There was a time during the late 1970's when that entrance was wide enough for a vehicle to drive through, travel between the breastworks and museum, and continue out to Seminole Avenue, a connector to U.S. 301. Although any cars and small trucks could traverse the path, allegedly its main purpose was to provide access for a small number of families who would otherwise need to go two miles out of their way in order to reach Seminole Avenue. But there were also the troublesome reports of serious safety issues related to that road, as the time that a pickup truck carrying a barrel with actively burning contents being driven so fast that it nearly collided with park visitors who were making their way from museum to breastworks. Something had to be done.

Park Superintendent Lt. Dal Myers went through the usual chain of command and finally managed to communicate his concerns to Ney Landrum, Director of Division of Recreation and

Parks of the Florida Department of Natural Resources (DNR). That resulted in Landrum arranging for prisoners from Zephyrhills Correctional Institution to construct a twenty-foot-wide split rail fence across the road so as to better protect the spot where Dade's soldiers had met their demise. For good measure, the fence was extended along the east side almost all the way down to the north park entrance, from which point vehicles were redirected to the recreational areas. As an added safety feature, the DNR had a small rise built in that portion of the remaining road near the visitor center, since it was now part of the park's internal loop road.

Myers died the night that the fencing was completed and his widow, Jean, along with Frank Laumer and others, felt forced to defend that fence from Sumter County officials who claimed that visitors would enjoy the convenience of viewing the battlefield from their vehicles, not to mention making things easier for the handicapped. At a meeting to which fence supporters were not invited, County Judge Jack Drawdy convinced Ney Landrum to agree to a removal of the fence. When she learned of that decision, Jean Myers said that the State would "have to take it down over me."

Looking for a way to block the logjam, Landrum wrote to the county attorney, Randall N. Thornton, advising the county to seek a 25-foot right-of-way at the park's east property line from the State so that a two-lane straightaway could be constructed. A county commissioner had even secured a promise from Joe Webb, owner of the property adjacent to the park's eastern border, to donate such a strip for roadbuilding purposes, thus bypassing the Park Service all together.

Jean Myers took a clever tack by contacting the federal government. Writing to the Heritage Conservation and Recreation Service, she inquired, "Isn't it against the law to build a new road within five hundred feet of a designated National Landmark?" It

Chapter 4: The Second Dade Massacre

took more than two months to receive a reply, but when one came from Ronald M. Greenberg, Acting Chief of the National Register Division, it was not what she expected. Greenberg wrote, "…should (road) construction proceed, the impact of the road on the integrity of the historic features of the battlefield may be substantial. In that case, this office would have to consider the revocation of the property's designation as a national historic landmark."

Before the end of 1980, no new road had been or would be built, since Mr. Webb had rescinded his offer and Landrum, becoming weary of the entire matter, decided to leave things as they were. A sign directed motorists to use only the northside road that passed under the iron entrance gate. Had it turned out otherwise, with traffic bisecting the critical focus of the park, drivers would be permitted to, in the words of reenactor Jerry Dean, "zoom over the very ground on which they spilled their blood (and be) an insult to their memory."[11]

The Second Dade Massacre

On July 4th, 1938, Ernest Burleigh Simmons, 65, member of the Florida Historical Society and frequent newspaper contributor of articles on Florida history based on his personal research and observations, visited the Independence Day celebration at Dade Memorial Park. Three days later, the *Tampa Times* published his letter to the editor that was titled, "Historical Errors?" In it, Simmons expressed his disappointment that not one of the "politician-speakers" paid any reference to the bloody massacre of 1835. He was critical of one speaker's inability to provide accurate historical dates at least four different times, and even decried J.C.B. Koonce's mistakes of putting Sioux war bonnets on the heads of his Indian statuary and for making his figure of Osceola stiffly straight in spite of historians of the early nineteenth century having described the storied leader as being "slightly hump-backed." He admonished future "writers and carvers" to portray "a more accurate history of (Dade's Battle) unless we prefer romantic error to truth." Simmons' chastisements might be considered to be one of the opening salvos in another battle that still lay almost four decades ahead.[12]

The Bicentennial of the United States was eagerly anticipated as a patriotic celebration in which the entire nation would be involved. It was the responsibility and duty of leaders at all levels of government and supporters of all historic sites to make plans for special events as well as to engage in a general sprucing-up to promote a resurgence of national pride, especially as the country was still recovering from the aftermath of Watergate. And so it was for the Department of Natural Resources.

The DNR plan for Dade Battlefield was to restore the appearance of the actual battle site to what it was in 1835. Many changes would be necessary in order to accomplish that goal, including closing the park's southern entrance road that was deemed hazardous to visitors by running right through the battleground, installing a culvert pipe to disguise the presence of a World War I-era drainage ditch, and removing nonnative shrubbery in favor of palmetto scrub and longleaf pine. The playground would have to be moved farther from the place of battle, and the ballfield, shuffleboard facility and much-praised tennis courts would be removed altogether, since the activities they provided were inconsistent with a historical site. James Cook, Chief of Park Operations, said that the DNR was hoping to make the recreation areas secondary to historical awareness and proper attention being paid to the memorial aspect of the park.[13]

Being aware of the affection for the park that was held by several generations of the local populace, state officials offered, as a courtesy, to meet with Sumter County commissioners to apprise them of their plans. That meeting took place on the park grounds

Chapter 4: The Second Dade Massacre

in late July of 1975. In attendance were County Commissioners Mike Lovett, Melvin Carter, and Bill Wing. Circuit Court Clerk C. Burton Marsh and DNR representatives John Feaster, Mike Bullock and Jim Stevenson joined in. Dade Memorial Park manager Carl Parks was also there. Bullock, Chief Bureau Design Planner and Stevenson, Park Programs Bureau Chief, did most of the talking, which was surprisingly well-received by the Sumter officials.

Four months later, Bullock was quoted as having said, "Well, there was a newspaper reporter there that day and I guess he wrote it up and they (Commissioners) started getting local calls." The protests to which he referred convinced DNR officials to address the Bushnell public directly and an informational meeting was scheduled for September of 1975. The meeting was conducted by representatives of the Division of Recreation and Parks in the Sumter County Courthouse. Finding themselves thrust into what Stevenson later described as "The Second Dade Massacre," the State officials gave a very well-prepared and professional presentation of the rationale and prospective benefits of the proposed changes, only to find their points (and even themselves) denounced by many speakers among the citizens packing the courtroom and overflowing into the hall and stairs.

One feared that returning to a virgin land appearance would result in rattlesnakes becoming the park's primary visitors. He even threatened to bring in his own tractor to mow down the high weeds and grasses. The presenters were told that while they may be plant experts, they didn't know anything about how important the park had been to Sumter Countians as a recreational destination. Broward Miller, former Sumter school superintendent, expressed the outrage of many present at the assault on "their little park." The *Sumter County Times* editor, Glen Wilson, Jr., compared the spectacle to a "subdued lynching." The sole support for the state officials was voiced by Frank Laumer, later (1979) quoted in that same newspaper as having said, "This is a battle site, not a Bushnell park."

The state delegation went home and met with others in order to re-think what could be done, while the people of Bushnell remained steadfast in their convictions. Nothing happened for five months until Ney Landrum visited the battlefield in a "spirit of compromise" according to Broward Miller. Eventually, the south road would be closed to traffic (except when it benefited the park in routing crowds during events), sporting courts and the ball field were eliminated, and the playground was moved westward to an area better suited for children's safety. The drainage ditch, however, is still there and the look of the grounds is what Jim Stevenson called "selective trimming," i.e., mowing the breastworks area and the Fort King Trail but allowing the surrounding spaces more freedom to grow. And the park's place in history became its primary feature that is expressed to visitors.[14]

The Statue

As chairman of the Dade Memorial Park Advisory Council, Sumter County School Superintendent Henry Broward Miller was patiently waiting, shears in hand, for Doctors Hanna and Grobman to finish speaking, his cue to cut the ceremonial ribbon that officially opened the new museum for public view on Independence Day of 1957. The mid-19th century soldier statue on duty between the two museum entries had only recently been removed from his elevated post of thirty-five years when the sixteen-foot stone and mortar monument had been demolished. Newly elected State Representative E.C. Rowell of Webster was overheard sharing with Miller the story of the old soldier's recent journey. It seemed that his removal from the pedestal had been intended to continue somewhere beyond the park's boundaries to parts unknown. "But the people of Sumter County," according to a nearby reporter's

Chapter 4: The Second Dade Massacre

witness, "would not see it any other way and demanded that their tall soldier from the past be assigned to this post." And the people got their way, since the soldier would stand guard right there for another four decades.[15]

No other Dade Park-related controversial issue has stirred the blood of Sumter Countians over time as much as unwanted change being proposed by persons beyond their borders. The ferocity of opposition against altering the park's appearance was initially such a shock to state officials that, although not abandoned, plans for such action were delayed for years. Since the most vocal resistance came from older residents, a strategy of biding time while gradually attempting to change public opinion took hold. But a nagging problem festering for years that became the flashpoint of the overall struggle was the soldier statue installed at the beginning of Dade Memorial Park.

Since that first official appearance on July 4, 1922, the bronze soldier, standing and holding a musket by its barrel, had engendered respect and, especially, affection among many local park visitors. Six feet tall, with a handlebar mustache and steely-eyed straight-ahead gaze, this work of metallurgy was quickly adopted by his fans as "Major Dade," the silent sentinel who was always on duty. By the time the State finally assumed daily management of the park, research had revealed mistakes in the old soldier's appearance.

At the time of its casting, images of U.S. Army uniforms of the Second Seminole War period were seldom seen. In fact, when patriotic murals were created depicting the progression of uniforms from 1776 to the present, the only one shown flanked between the War of 1812 and Civil War was from the Mexican War. Perhaps artists took the erroneous position that the Florida conflict was only a regional matter, even though over half of all men who wore military uniforms in the country were involved in what, up to then, was the longest war of any kind in American history. Or maybe they were just uninformed. Regardless of the reason, J.C.B. Koonce approved a rendition of a soldier that seemed right to him, except that it was that of a Union enlisted man of the Civil War, flat-topped "Kepi" cap and all. Dade's men were issued the 1833 leather forage cap, a taller, double-peaked head covering (See Fig. 33).[16]

A 1983 survey at the park tallied the most asked questions. Number one was, "Where is the ladies room?" but coming in at second place was, "Why does the state have a Civil War statue at a Seminole War park?" In-person questions were frequent, but there was also a noticeable quantity of letters written that left a tangible record. An example of these is one from an active duty Army captain referencing, "that anachronistic Union soldier" and then offering his assistance in contacting U.S. Representative Bill Chappell of Ocala with a petition to remedy the matter.

Knowledgeable visitors had made the statue an object of ridicule and had criticized the State for not knowing any better, according to retired Dade museum guide Winnie Murphy in 1991. That same year, Park manager Jeff Montgomery admitted, "It's awkward for us (and) makes us look ignorant." He opined that all this was an old story, and the only reason no State action had been taken with the statue is because doing so would greatly anger some local residents.

Dade Battlefield Society president Sheila Mann suggested keeping the statue only if the hat could be sliced off and replaced with a more authentic one. But decapitation and full head/hat replacement would be needed, since Army regulations in the 1830's required soldiers to be clean shaven. Elizabeth Ehrbar, Museum Exhibit Design Supervisor for the Bureau of Biological and Interpretive Services, picked up on this by investigating how much it would cost to replace the head with a new beardless one sporting

Chapter 4: The Second Dade Massacre

the proper cap. She was quoted a price of $6,000 to accomplish the task but found that to be far beyond her budget.

None of this was received well by the older folks in town, some of whom witnessed the figure's original installation. In a 1981 letter to James A. Cook, Chief of Park Operations, Secretary of Sumter County Historical Society Irene S. Miller wrote, "We strongly feel that removal of the soldier would cause much concern among those who have supported the park for many years." She went on to say that if the soldier is so inauthentic, the State could replace it with a new, more acceptable model. One of the most prominent dissenters, Broward Miller, was already on record as stating, "The authenticity of the statue isn't important anyway. Besides, I think the state just wants to get rid of it." Three years later, he was still going strong. "The citizens of Sumter County accept the statue as being from the proper era and want it to remain," he said in 1994. "The statue is so much a part of the Dade Battlefield Memorial Park that local residents are willing to fight to keep it." In an Associated Press release, C. Burton Marsh, a man who traced his Sumter roots back to his great-great grandparents, made a comment that was hard to forget. He stated, "If the soldier was standing out there in bloomers, it wouldn't make any difference – don't change that statue."

Figure 35: Broward Miller.

The most innovative resolution offer had come from Jon Dodrill, who presented it to the park and to the Dade Battlefield Society. He proposed that a plaque should be placed near the statue that first praised the work of Judge J.C.B. Koonce for commissioning it. Further statements would refer to it as a Civil War soldier who represented "a memorial not only to the personnel who fell in battle on this site December 28, 1835, but to the 63 Sumter County residents who gave their lives in the defense of their country during other wars." Dodrill brought this proposal to Broward Miller as they met in front of the statue. Mr. Miller, although cordial and possessed of an even temperament, read the line, "Civil War era soldier" and refused to review any of the verbiage that followed. The plaque was never produced.

Although the exact date has not been determined, sometime between 1994 and 1998 the statue was quietly transferred to the tool cage of the pole barn in the non-public access area of the park. In recent years there emerged an idea that perhaps the Department of Environmental Protection may be persuaded to find a place for the old soldier in their collections facility. In the very least, it has existed for more than a century and represents the beginning of the early park, thus justifying it as a candidate for preservation for that reason alone.[17]

The saga continues.

Public Relations 4'x6' foam board designed by the author, 2021. Produced by Tampa Type/Print.
Provided by the Author

Chapter Five
THE HARMONIOUS EXPANSION

*"Dade Park is too important,
too historical and too beautiful to be neglected."*
A.D. Powers, 1926.

A little over one year after his first visit to Dade Battlefield, Frank Laumer set out to lead a group consisting of two of his children, ages twelve and fourteen, six friends, and his ten-year-old collie Amos on a hike of sixty miles that traced the path of Brevet Major Dade's command from Fort Brooke to the Dade site. Burton Marsh met the finishers at the end of their journey and told them that he hoped an annual battle reenactment would evolve from their trek. It would take more than two decades of additional research, publication of a book and several articles, and the collaboration of a host of other interested parties before the Clerk's wish would be realized, but a new era of scholarly investigation on Dade and his story had begun.[1]

Laumer's drive to learn even more about the 1835 battle was increasing. Through his comrade-in-arms on the recent trek, Attorney and Florida Historical Society board member William Goza, a small group of other members professing interest in archaeological authentication was assembled. This rapid development helped persuade Dade Battlefield Memorial Park Superintendent John Hale to request permission from the Florida Park Service for a dig of the breastwork gravesites – no easy accomplishment itself.

Permission was granted, however with only a three-day window for completion.

March 6 and 7, 1964, were days of great activity at a gravesite near the breastwork's west end. The east end graves' investigation was delayed until the fourth of April. A hole was started and the dirt removed was sifted through ¼ inch screen wire mesh. Digging was continued until the outlines of two trenches were seen, and it was agreed that these were two graves in which the enlisted men had been buried. The second excavation was performed in a similar manner that yielded similar, albeit fewer, manufactured items. Nothing associated with higher ranking officers was identified. Over five hundred artifacts were uncovered, about seventy per cent of which consisted of buttons. Twenty-five rifle balls were unearthed, some of which were flattened by hitting human bone. There were also buckles, pens, nails, and assorted teeth or portions thereof, of both human and animal origins. A sampling of some of these items remains to this day in the park's museum, while the majority were sent out for cleaning and further examination to the Florida State Museum in Gainesville. Most never made their way back to the park.[2]

Newsworthy activities that were connected to Dade Battlefield were becoming more numerous and Sumter County commissioners were taking notice. The Commission issued a proclamation that exhorted all its citizens to observe Pioneer Memorial Day by "gathering on the hallowed grounds of Dade Memorial Park, at the prescribed hour, to take part in this memorial occasion." Despite no "prescribed hour" having been mentioned, there indeed was a gathering at which people were welcomed and heard presentations form five different speakers, one of whom read an eyewitness account of the grisly scene when the first troops arrived almost fifty-six days after the battle had ended. Courtesy of the South Sumter High School Band, a recording of the funeral march music

Chapter 5: The Harmonious Expansion

performed on that day was played for the guests. The announced hope was that an annual all-day event would ensue.[3]

J.C.B. Koonce's original 1919 goal to have the Dade site named a national park would never be realized. But in 1974 at least some positive Federal recognition occurred when Dade Battlefield was officially designated a National Historic Landmark by the National Park Service. The certificate and plaque characterized it as possessing "national significance in commemorating the history of the United States of America." Soon after this new source of pride was installed, events that led to the aforementioned Second Dade Massacre took place and the need for cooler heads was manifested.[4]

On Sunday, January 8, 2017, Frank Laumer, age 89, was making his final address to the assembly of Dade's Battle reenactors prior to his taking the field one last time as the ghost of Ransom Clark, survivor of the 1835 rout.

"My first visit to this park, this battlefield, was in 1962, fifty-five years ago. I had never heard of Major Dade, knew nothing of Seminole Indians, or something called the Seminole War. They only had a pamphlet. I began to research. Eighteen years later, in 1980, a program was planned for December 28th. I was asked to speak. I've been speaking ever since."[5]

The person who asked for Laumer's participation in that program was Jon Dodrill, a new hire at the Department of Natural Resources. Dade Park manager Lieutenant Wayne Edwards had suggested a 145th anniversary Dade Battlefield Day, and Dodrill's interest was piqued. He was told of Laumer's expertise on the subject, so great that he had been hailed as the authority on all things related to the Dade massacre. The emphasis was to be on interpretation, not just a show for entertainment's sake. Jon had the resources, and Frank had the knowledge and passion for the subject.

Situated forty miles south of Dade Battlefield is Hillsborough River State Park and the recently reconstructed Second Seminole

War cantonment of Fort Foster. One park ranger from there, as well as two volunteers, all attired as 1830s soldiers, joined Laumer and Dodrill along with John Mahon and William Goza, the current and past presidents of the Florida Historical Society, to present the program. An audience of approximately three hundred braved cold weather similar to that encountered by Dade's men to sit and stand around the concrete breastworks while listening to the presentations. Of particular interest was the first-person account so emotionally performed by Laumer as he enacted the part of a uniformed and severely wounded Ransom Clark, one of only two survivors who made it back to civilization after a stunning defeat. This was the beginning of what would hopefully become an annual event through which generations of people would be able to learn of the significance of events that had been far too often overlooked.[6]

Figure 36: Bill Goza speaking at first commemoration (Dec. 28, 1980).

So encouraged by the public reception the first time out, Jon Dodrill planned a very elaborately detailed program for the second Dade Battlefield Day that greatly increased its previous scope.

Chapter 5: The Harmonious Expansion

Along with the participants who were present in 1980, this one was to include an actual Seminole speaker claiming to be a descendant of Osceola, as well as Indian portrayers, a thirty-member high school wind ensemble, a kitchen crew, active military and militia camps complete with operating cook fires and food, a musket volley, a speaker describing conditions for African-Americans in 1830s Florida, and a local reverend performing an invocation.[7] Yet despite all the preparation and the fact that all participants, speakers, and many visitors showed up, the Florida Park Service representatives cancelled due to unexpectedly deplorable weather conditions. In a follow-up letter of apology to Dr. John Mahon, Dodrill assured him that the rescheduled program of February fourteenth "will go on even if I have to drive the nails to build the Ark so that everyone can speak from it."[8]

A different slant was provided for the third outing of January 2, 1983. On the previous day, a group of dedicated living historians marched, as Dade-era soldiers, from the southern to northern limits of both Zephyrhills and Dade City, being transported by vans between the two. This was a New Year's Day effort to call public attention to the upcoming Dade Battlefield Day, after which reenactors were then driven to the park to set up camp for the next day's program.[9]

Figure 37: Frank Laumer speaking (Feb.14, 1982).

Although little remembered today, in 1984 there was a first iteration of Dade Battlefield Society prior to the one that is well known today. It grew from a group that had formed to celebrate the Bushnell Centennial, an event that later morphed into the Bushnell Fall Festival. The thought was that a group comprised of spirited residents coupled with historians and reenactors could benefit the park by becoming a unified organization and central base for conducting the annual commemorations. A major player in this effort was Marsha Woodard, daughter of the park superintendent who served from the mid-1940's to the early 1950's. Her aim was to break through the barrier that existed between local people and the State. It was a valiant effort that, unfortunately, once again exposed disagreement between Bushnell and Sumter residents and history experts from farther reaches. The group disbanded almost before it started. Nevertheless, the popular commemorative event continued to grow and to experiment with new features designed to add to the public's enjoyment and, ultimately, its learning.[10]

There were two commemorative days in 1984, one in mid-January and the other in late December. Of the first, Museum Guide Winnie Murphy said, "It's not a reenactment, it's a living history." By the time the later day was marked, that statement could no longer be made since December 29, 1984 included something billed as a "Soldier/Indian Skirmish." But by the 150th anniversary of Dade's Battle on December 28, 1985, a full-scale battle reenactment was performed for the first time. Despite being in the midst of a $230,000 renovation project, on that day the park welcomed over seven thousand spectators who observed the detailed scenario-driven line of march and a borrowed horse-drawn cannon being put to use.

The record-setting audience, gathered behind a rope line stretching three hundred feet over what until recently had been a ball field, observed the pageant happening before them at and beyond the tree line. Guests seated in lawn chairs or directly on the ground occupied a few prime viewing spots, while the vast majority

Chapter 5: The Harmonious Expansion

stood, jockeying for position, in order to better view and photograph the drama they were witnessing. The combatants pretended to fight in an area of Dade Battlefield State Historic Site that more closely resembled the palmetto and pine barren encountered by the real 1835 adversaries, rather than the mostly oak hammock that now occupied the nearby actual battle location. Nearly three hundred actors portrayed the original one hundred ten troops and one hundred eighty Seminoles and their allies. The State of Florida, Bushnell Kiwanis Club and other local groups sponsored the free event, and noon and six o'clock dinners were available for three dollars each.[11]

Figure 38: Reenactment audience (2019).

Wayne Edwards recognized the continuing need for a stable group of community members that would try once again to organize for support of the reenactment and other park activities. He made the case anew and Marsha Woodard, along with local residents Ginger Bell, Sheila Mann and others, were encouraged to help in such a way that eventually led to the June 8, 1987, chartering of a new Dade Battlefield Society. This non-profit corporation would operate as the park's Citizen Support Organization (CSO), and immediately took on the planning and production of the annual commemoration from that time forward. Fresh funding was a critical need, and the CSO planned and managed the first annual "Old Fashioned Day in the Park," an event that was attended by approximately two thousand five hundred visitors. Historians and living historians spoke and demonstrated. There were mule wagon rides, bands, singers, dancers, carnival games, a precision horse drill team, and plenty of food and drink. An evening beauty pageant closed the day with Stephanie Rogers named, "Miss Dade Battlefield Society." The event's net profit was $5,122.13. A second effort one year later would double that amount.

The initial commemoration for which the Society was responsible, in January of 1988, became the first to be extended to both weekend days. There was a Saturday skirmish and a full, scripted battle on Sunday afternoon. A feature during the following December, as a lead-in to the reenactment, was a Society-sponsored trek from Tampa to Dade Battlefield, once again led by Frank Laumer as he had done twenty-five years before. This new group of living historians going with him reached the park on the first day of that year's event.[12]

The tenth reenactment, in 1989, marked the beginning of the present-day pattern of conducting a battle on each of the two days. It also coincided with the Smithsonian's loan of an officer's sword that had been salvaged from the Dade battle site by a member of the force of nine hundred eighty soldiers who came in 1836 to bury the dead of that engagement.[13]

Each successive annual reenactment could be noted for its accompanying additions and alterations, most of which being for the better. Over the years since then, poor weather occasionally marred the event, while at other times an unexpectedly high number of visitors showed up. As it went, Dade's Battle Reenactment

Chapter 5: The Harmonious Expansion

and Trade Fair of 2015 was close to average in terms of participation and visitor attendance and therefore will be used as an example.

Figure 39: Preparing to fire at the enemy at Reenactment of Dade's Battle (2019).

Figure 40: Seminoles Daniel Tommie and Pedro Zepeda (2017).

There was much to see and do each day prior to the 2:00 PM battle. Seminole and Seminole-portraying families in their camps showed how they conducted their daily lives. Cooking, mending, tool-making, caring for livestock. Visitors could test their prowess at tomahawk throwing, too. The soldiers were outside their tents, cleaning their muskets and drilling in proper military fashion. Over at the nearby breastworks (made more authentic twenty-one years previously by having actual pine logs replace the misaligned Koonce-era concrete ones), small groups gathered to hear author John Missall tell "The Seminole Side of the Story." Closer to the lodge building were over four dozen craft demonstrators and period-dressed sutlers hawking appropriate sets of wares. Food vendors offered sandwiches, ice cream, southern soul food, and Indian frybread. Children could play organized pioneer games. There were exhibitors from local non-profits and, on Sunday, even an ordained minister conducting a church service straight out of the nineteenth century.

Figure 41: Frank Laumer as the ghost of Ransom Clark (2017).

As a professional Florida folk singer started to perform, over two thousand five hundred visitors who attended the two-day event were drawn to an area southwest of the trade fair where seventy-one soldiers would do battle with forty-two warriors. The forty-five-minute struggle was fully scripted and narrated, both by a uniformed figure portraying the spirit of battle survivor Ransom Clark as well as a Seminole actor taking the role of Chief Jumper. The audience was seated in metal bleachers and personal lawn chairs on a graded mound, completed twenty-five years before, located in the former softball outfield. An authentically-reproduced six pounder cannon, purchased by the CSO, fired multiple rounds as it had each year since 2003. Select pines were felled and stacked three logs high by the soldiers in a desperate attempt to provide cover against anticipated additional attacks. But the battle reenactment's end was the same as it had been for twenty-nine years: all soldiers gone save three who were cautiously waiting to hide, limp, and crawl away.

Chapter 5: The Harmonious Expansion

Two buglers rose from the field of still bodies to play a haunting echo-effect version of Taps.

The call to "Resurrect!" went out, cuing all reenactors, military and Indian, to reappear and fire musket and rifle salutes in honor of the brave men and women of all of our nation's armed conflicts who sacrificed for the causes in which they believed.

With all the support and notoriety that Dade's Battle reenactment has enjoyed over the years, perhaps it is not surprising that the park staff and Dade Battlefield Society members have often received inquiries about producing a large Civil War event. While a Union and Confederate encounter would undoubtedly receive much attention, permission for such an undertaking has never been granted by the Florida Park Service since there was never any military engagement anywhere near Bushnell during that chapter of American history. But there *is* a connection, and a strong one at that, between Dade Park and the nation's involvement in the Second World War. One wag even quipped that, given the Army's "occupation" of the park for more than two years in the 1940s, it would be better named Early Warning Radar Historic State Park.

Dade Battlefield State Historic Site hosted its first World War II Day in August of 1998, but by the time it was expanded into a two-day affair in 2012 both reenactors and guests were lobbying to reschedule future outings to a cooler time of year. The

Figure 42: American WWII soldier reenactors (March, 2015).

World War II Commemorative Weekend held in March, 2015, involved eight hundred nine visitors who were able to interact with Allied and Axis reenactors having authentic camps, equipment, and motorized vehicles. There was still a 2:00 PM skirmish staged in sight of the viewing mound, only this time the setting was Occupied France of 1944 and the eighty soldiers included American infantrymen and German paratroopers.[14]

Figure 43: Samantha Gordon, Shannon Werner, and Sue Blakeman perform as the Andrews Sisters at WWII variety show (2015).

Beginning around 2009, the number and variety of new programs and activities at the park greatly increased, in part as a reaction to twice-threatened closures due to state budget shortfalls, but more often as an attempt to re-establish the park as a community resource as well as a big event destination. As author A.D. Powers had penned three quarters of a century earlier, "There is one thing certain. Dade Park is too important, too historical and too beautiful to be neglected."

Military services at both the Federal and State national guard levels recognize the importance of studying the asymmetric warfare characteristics of Dade's Battle, and they make regular trips to the park to learn more about it. Beginning with the Florida National Guard and continuing with regular visits by officers working with the National Defense University's Joint Forces Staff College, park staff and CSO volunteers extend participant learning by interpreting the different perspectives of soldier and Seminole during their long-ago era of conflict. They speak of uniformed, disciplined military personnel and native fighters who used the environment when engaging an enemy force. Major General Emmett Titshaw,

Chapter 5: The Harmonious Expansion

Jr., Adjutant General of the Florida National Guard, commented upon "how the Seminoles capitalized on their strengths and by paying attention to signs that were out there." Comparing the experience gained by his officers with the past, he said, "Whether it's 1835 here or outside the wire in Afghanistan, those things are the same."

Figure 44: Staff ride principals (2012). Major General Emmett R. Titshaw, Jr., Board Member Steve Creamer, Board President Steve Rinck, Board Member John Griffin, Florida National Guard Command Historian Lt. Col. (Ret.) Greg Moore, Regional Training Institute Commander Col. Grant Slaydon.

Youth education and citizenship is encouraged through field trips, quality outreach programs, sponsoring of scholarships, and creation of the Dade Pioneers for elementary school children and Dade's Youth for teens interested in earning volunteer hours while allowing them to become Dade Battlefield Society members. The community Haunted Event each October, classic car exhibits, wildlife programs, music concerts, art shows and evening outdoor

Figure 45: Day Campers at "One Room Schoolhouse" (2015).

Figure 46: Junior Archer at Pioneer Day Camp (2015).

Figure 47: Dade Pioneers learning about artillery (2021).

movies have been enjoyed along with more opportunities for personal growth experiences such as guided nature walks, trash-to-treasure crafting, geo-caching, and the entertaining "Incredible Edibles." There are dozens of unique classes for park patrons that continue to be offered regularly. Making grapevine wreaths, pine needle baskets and wild fruit jelly attract participants, as does pinecone flower art, upcycled paper and glass arts and the ever-popular Dutch oven cooking. Week-long pioneer and nature day camps provide summer learning adventures for elementary-aged children, and other central Florida groups hold their meetings and events at the park more frequently than before.[15]

New events create awareness of the park and continue to build attendance. Surveys indicate large numbers of people, some from as close as Bushnell, are discovering that Dade Park exists and is a wonderful place to spend the day. Such reality translates into benefits for the greater community; during the park's 2021/22 fiscal year, its activities supported eighty-nine local jobs and had an economic impact of $6,783,996.

Chapter 5: The Harmonious Expansion

As of this writing, the eighty acres purchased in 1921 has been expanded to one hundred twenty acres thanks to a May 29, 2020 acquisition by the State. That means since the first time in a century, within park boundaries lies the entire field of battle, including the pond into which victorious Seminoles deposited the cannon that took part in the old conflict. But in spite of all the changes the land has endured, generations of faithful supporters continue to enjoy celebrating Independence Day at what many still call, "our little park." Contemporary staff have re-invigorated the time-honored tradition with the annual Patriotic Family Fun Day held every July third. The dreams of J.C.B. Koonce, the fervent wishes of Bushnell citizens, and the responsible stewardship of State officials co-exist now in a lasting harmony. The land that is Dade Battlefield Historic State Park welcomes all. [16]

Figure 48: Old Majestic Oak (2021).

Informational kiosk at Dade Battlefield Historic State Park, installed in 2023 and provided by *Explore Sumter!*
Photo provided by the Author.

Appendix A

Stories of Personal Experiences at the Park

When beginning research for this book, the author decided to begin by interviewing selected residents from Bushnell and its environs. When potential interviewees were contacted for appointments, all of them agreed to participate and looked forward to seeing their names in print, and a few have already been quoted in previous pages. All but one individual, Burton Marsh, have been personally interviewed by the author.

Burton Marsh

Burton described how he and the other boys caught fish in the canal that flowed through the park. He brought his father's old croaker tote sack along because it was supplied with meal, lard, salt, a frying pan and knives that came in handy when the boys would clean, fry, and consume their catch right on the spot. A little further down the canal was a swimming hole of which they made good use regularly. And they did not get in trouble with their mothers since there was no one to see them jump in after having left their clothes on the bank.

Burton's friend Doris Woodward added something humorous regarding the soldiers who camped at the park during World War II. In those days of free-range cattle, one cow managed to stick her head into one of the tents at night and wake up a soldier by licking his face.[1]

Marsha Woodard Perkins

Marsha never lived on the park property, but her parents, Edwin and Nell Woodard, did during the eight years when Ed served as caretaker. She nevertheless has plenty of stories about Dade Park, including the time her dad reported seeing a spirit on the property and came out with his hunting dogs in an attempt to track it down. Ed's brother-in-law Vernon Huff preceded him as caretaker.

Marsha is a lifelong resident of Bushnell, and from the age of thirty became a strong advocate for Dade Park. She helped form both the first and second iterations of Dade Battlefield Society, and as treasurer was the catalyst that helped the second one to benefit the park successfully. Her biggest surprise related to the park was that, during the second Laumer-led march from Tampa to Bushnell in 1988, she met fellow marcher Steve Perkins; ten months later they were married.[2]

Figure 49: Cousins Marsha Woodard and Frank Hamilton (1988).

Frank Hamilton

Frank is Marsha's cousin and served Sumter County as tax collector for thirty-six years, retiring in 2006. At Dade Battlefield, he well remembers playing in the drainage ditch as a kid. South of the oldest picnic pavilion was a 2-restroom building that was elevated on a mound of the same native rock as other structures around the park. Each side was just big enough to accommodate a toilet and lavatory. "It looked creepy," he said.

John W. Outlaw

Johnny Outlaw was Marsha Perkins' uncle by marriage, and he lived with her and Steve during the last few months of his 95 years of life. The author visited with him at his Inverness home when he was 92, where he spoke about visiting the Centennial Commemoration as a teenager.

Figure 50: Johnny Outlaw (2014).

Johnny had heard about Marsha's Aunt Almarene and showed up at a church picnic with the intention of meeting her. The event was at Dade Memorial Park, and he introduced himself by using an ax and a butcher knife. That is, Almarene had borrowed them from her brother, the park caretaker, to cut logs and slice hot dog buns. Johnny volunteered to do those chores; they got married a few months later. Referring to Dade Memorial, he told me, "The park was a choice place to go in Sumter County."

Josephine Strong-Simmons

The author spoke with Josephine when she was ninety years of age. She moved to Bushnell in 1953 during her education career that spanned 51 years. She was the first female principal to serve in Sumter County.

In 1941, 10th grader Josephine came to a barbecue at Dade Battlefield at the invitation of her best girlfriend. She had to ride in the rumble seat of the car being driven by the girl's boyfriend. Josephine ended up marrying the boyfriend.

The road to the park entrance was paved to the gate, then dirt after coming in. There were statues peppered all through the woods that were made of concrete and hand painted by Judge Koonce. Many were of Indians but there were also quite a few of soldiers, especially in and around the reproduction breastworks.

Martin Steele

He remembers going to Dade Park for school field trips in the late fifties, touring the museum and seeing a number of visually fascinating statues. When he was attending junior college, he played tennis at the park since there were no courts where he lived in Webster. He thought that the Gatling guns that flanked the concrete breastworks were really cool and could not understand why they were later removed. Martin's grandfather was a blacksmith and had made the wagon wheels for those guns.

Martin's high school Agriculture teacher brought students to the park for FFA forestry units. He taught them "timber cruising" to determine the height and diameter of trees and to estimate board feet of timber.

Appendices

Ginger Bell Realmuto

A former president of Dade Battlefield Society, Ginger told the author, "Bushnell is very unique and so is Dade Battlefield Park. You have a different feeling when you come in. It's not just the park to come in and have a picnic. My husband-to-be and I came here for our wedding pictures."[3]

Gayle Hunt

Except for his United States Navy service during World War II, Gayle lived his entire 97 years in the same house in which he was born in 1926. It's in Bushnell, on the southeast corner of Seminole and West Avenues. His father, Enos, was the first caretaker at Dade Park. He had a twelve-inch female alligator named Joe to which he fed pancakes every morning. When her size became more of a concern he took her to Homosassa Springs.

Figure 51: Gayle Hunt, U.S. Navy, during World War II.

The Hunts were a large family and seemed to be involved in most of the town's business. Gayle's Uncle Charlie Hunt had a filling station in town that was staffed by members of his family who needed work. From time to time, that included Gayle's Uncle Alva ("Alvie") who was on J. Edgar Hoover's "Ten Most Wanted" list in 1937. Alva and his brother-in-law and fellow gang member Hugh Gant terrorized southeastern banks and by 1938 the FBI elevated their status, collectively, to "Public Enemy Number One." Gayle said that his Uncle Alvie used to pop into town unannounced and take him and his friend Sam Coverston out fishing, always having plenty of money for bait. When he was released after completing a long prison sentence, Alva opened a Shell station at the southwest corner of US 301 and Seminole Avenue.

Gayle knew most of Bushnell's prominent citizens. He characterized Ralph Collins as "a nice man," and when asked about J.C.B. Koonce he said, "He took care of the park like it was his living room." Gayle's younger cousin Scrammy Hunt lived right next to the park, and when the Army took it over in 1943, the guards let him (at age nine) shoot their guns.[4]

Figure 52: Sam Coverston with South Sumter HS driver education students (ca. 1969).

Appendices

Sam Coverston

The late Sam Coverston was just a plethora of facts about Dade Park, Bushnell and Sumter County. His family arrived in Bushnell in 1925 during Florida boom times. The town was so crowded with newcomers that the city commission gave approval to set up camp at Dade Memorial Park for any of the pilgrims needing a place to stay, and for an indefinite span of time. Counting backwards from his March of 1927 birth, Sam firmly believed that he was conceived on park property. He has memories of the park since he was five years old.

Battlefield Parkway is wide because it once was a 2-lane road with large oak trees in the middle. One of the trees had a Model T crank handle embedded in it, probably due to an accident. And in the early forties, a man hung himself in the park's gazebo.

Sam worked in the fields of real estate, insurance, and soil conservation, but his real passion was always teaching. He taught students in the subjects of history, civics, government, family agriculture and Drivers' Education. In the mid-sixties he would direct his Drivers' Ed students to pull into Dade Memorial Park in order to learn different skills. He set up concrete posts to teach parallel parking. Sam was also known to test the skills of his students by requiring them to drive in reverse through all the paved roads in the park. Of course, this had also been the time that Frank Laumer and others were performing archaeologic digs within the breastworks, and Sam the history teacher really enjoyed watching and later quizzing his students as to what they had observed and experienced. At about this same time, Sam and wife Marjorie were in a square dancing club that met weekly in Dade's Lodge.[5]

Appendix B

Four years after its official dedication, A.D. Powers wrote and published, "The DADE MASSACRE and Dade Memorial Park." Drawing from the written works of both Frederick Cubberly and J.C.B. Koonce, it was intended to serve two purposes: To introduce to and familiarize the public with the details of Dade's Battle and to encourage the new park's financial support to broaden and continue. The page below and the following seventeen is a reproduction of Power's booklet.

Appendices

THIS FENCE MARKS THE OLD TRAIL.

Dade Massacre and Dade Memorial Park
Written by A. D. Powers

Government Document No. 33

The United States Senate on the first session of the Sixty-seventh Congress ordered the printing of the story of the Dade Massacre, written by Frederick Cubberly, Attorney at Law, of Gainesville, Florida.

I am taking much information from this document, as it has the approval of the United States Senate, and must be as accurate as it is possible to find the information about this important event in history.

The story of the massacre of detachments from the First and Second Regiments of Artillery and Fourth Regiment of Infantry, of the United States Army was presented by Senator Duncan U. Fletcher, and ordered printed by the Committee on printing. It was printed by the Government Printing Office in nineteen-twenty one.

The artillery and infantry detachments were under the command of Major Francis L. Dade and the massacre occured on December the twenty-eighth, 1835.

Indians Did Not Want to Leave Florida

The Indians made a treaty with the United States Government at Paynes Landing that obligated them to leave Florida and settle west of the Mississippi River. A few of the chiefs were disposed to abide by the treaty, but they were divided and there was a general disturbed feeling in the year eighteen thirty-five.

General Wiley Thompson, the Indian Agent at Fort King, had many conferences with the Seminoles, and reported from time to time to the Washington officials, of their disinclination to abide by their treaty. He

Beyond the Battle

DRIVE IN DADE MEMORIAL PARK

really foresaw the danger that was impending.

Fort King was one of the important Government Forts in Florida and was located near the present site of Ocala.

The Indians wanted to abide by a former treaty made at Camp Moultrie, near St. Augustine, and the officials at Washington insisted on the new treaty.

It has been said that many of the Indians who were transported to Indian Territory made their way back to Florida. When asked why they came back they replied that there was no light wood in the new country. The Indians used pine knots as torches in their night wanderings, and for their ceremonial activities at night, and they could not carry on without the pine knots.

President Andrew Jackson Was Firm

President Jackson insisted on the Indians living up to their agreement to leave Florida and go to the new country and many of the Indian chiefs were equally firm in their determination to stay. The fact that there are some hundreds of Seminole Indians in Florida to this good day indicates that it would take more than a treaty to move them.

In a message dated February the sixteenth, eighteen thirty-five, directed to the Chiefs and warriors of the Seminole Indians in Florida, President Jackson used these words. "You know me, and you know I would not deceive you nor advise you to do anything that was unjust or injurious." "I tell you that you must go and that you will go. You have sold all your country. You have not a place as large as a blanket to sit down upon."

The Indians held councils at Fort King in March and April 1835. President Jackson's message was communicated to them and the situation was explained to the Indians by General Thompson, the Indian Agent.

General Duncan L. Clinch was in command in Florida. He and other experienced army officers argued with the Indians, all to no avail. The Indians were just as determined to

Appendices

THE UNFINISHED FORT WHERE DADE'S MEN FELL

stay as the Government was to move them west.

General Thompson Asked For Reinforcements

The Indians were sulky, and comparatively few of them came to Fort King during the summer. The parleys with the Indians were prolonged, but no agreement could be arrived at concerning when the Indians would consent to go. It was finally decided to begin moving them by force at the end of the year, or early in 1836.

General Thompson advised the Washington Government to send reinforcements before beginning the campaign of agression. The small force at Fort King was inadequate and combined with the force at Fort Brook there would still be insufficient men to carry out the Government's orders.

On numerous occasions General Thompson and other generals recommended the reinforcement of these two posts and especially of the post at Fort King.

Fort Brooke was located on Tampa Bay, near the present city of Tampa.

There was a trail known as the Fort King road from Fort Brooke to Fort King. The distance between these two posts was about a hundred miles. The road crossed numerous small streams between the posts and these were bridged with rough bridges.

Orders were given for detachments of the First and Second Artillery and Fourth Infantry to move from Key West by boat to Fort Brooke and then to march on to Fort King. Major Francis L. Dade was put in command of this ill-fated army.

Major Dade Begins his Last March

It was late in December that Major Dade and his command began their march from Fort Brooke on the Fort King trail. Travel was necessarily slow, but as the days passed nothing was heard of Major Dade and his men at Fort Brook and no word had reached Fort King.

Early in January a private soldier named Daniel F. Clarke crawled into

TUSTENUGGEE LODGE IN DADE PARK

Fort Brooke more dead than alive. He had seven wounds, and was weak from the loss of blood and the lack of food. He had crawled most of the way from the scene of the massacre, about eighty miles, to Fort Brooke.

One hundred and two privates and non-commissioned officers and eight officers left Fort Brook on December the twenty-fourth, the day before Christmas, and Daniel F. Clark and two others were the only ones ever seen alive again.

It is needless to say that the news that Clarke brought to Fort Brooke brought consternation into the United States officials as well as to the army. This unexpected attack awakened the authorities at Washington to the seriousness of the situation.

For the first time in the history of the United States, practically an entire command of trained and hardened soldiers had been exterminated by the Indians. The attack occurred in daylight, contrary to the usual Indian custom.

General Thompson Ambushed

On the same day of the Dade Massacre, Chief Osceola and a band of Indians appeared at Fort King. General Thompson and his aide, Lieutenant Smith, were walking near the agency buildings when they were ambushed and killed.

The Indians then looted the Sutler's store, and carried off large quantities of ammunition, liquor and stores. Osceola and his savages then departed along the trail to meet Micanopy and Alligator and their band, who had earlier in the day wiped out Major Dade and his entire command with the exception of three men.

Major Dade, A Seasoned Soldier

Major Dade was a veteran of the war of 1812. He was a brave and experienced soldier. He was aware of the unsettled condition of the country and of the dissatisfaction of the Indians. His detachment travelled with oxen as the means of transport and was necessarily slow.

Appendices

He had only one piece of artillery, a six pounder. This was also drawn by oxen. Clarke, the survivor, said Major Dade moved slowly and with caution, until he had crossed the Withlacoochee River; that he sent scouts ahead; that he made entrenched camps at night, cut trees for breastworks and took every precaution against attack.

The day before the attack the command had crossed the last river and had encamped for the night near a small lake about four miles south of the place where the attack occurred. On the morning of the twenty-eighth day of December, Major Dade assembled his command near the lake, and addressed them. The lake is now known as Dade's Breakfast Lake. It is the place where he and his men ate their last breakfast. He told them the most dangerous part of their journey was passed, and that they were nearing their destination. He told them that it would probably be the last day of their march, and it was. He said they would probably spend the night in Fort King.

Up until this last day he had advanced with caution, using flankers and advance guard. On the morning of December the twenty-eighth, having passed the thick swamps, and being only a day's march from his destination, he probably relaxed his vigilance. There was only a small advance guard. The weather was cold and the men were wearing their overcoats. The ammunition was in boxes under the buttoned overcoats.

CAPTAIN FRASER DIED ON THIS SPOT

Attacked Without Warning

Major Dade and Captain Fraser marched at the head of the column, close behind the advance guard. The men in double file followed. They were four miles north of the night camp on the lake, in the open pine woods, west of a small lake. The grass was tall and there were many clumps of saw palmetto. An ideal place for the murderous attack.

The Indians and a large number of their negro slaves were concealed in the grass and palmettoes. The command was marching slowly along the

Beyond the Battle

BRIDGE OVER THE CREEK IN DADE PARK

trail. The attack was unexpected. It was contrary to all methods of Indian warfare.

Chief Jumper gave a shrill war whoop. This was followed by a single shot by Chief Micanopy. Immediately a sheet of fire from the ambushed Indians poured into the unsuspecting soldiers. More than half the command fell at the first volley. The attack was well planned and the Indians' aim was nearly perfect. The Indians had evidently discussed and planned every detail.

Alligator Tells The Story

Halpatter-Tustenuggee, better known as Alligator, was present and one of the leading Chiefs engaged in the Massacre. Later he told the story of the massacre, and it is probably as nearly correct as an Indian could tell it.

Alligator said that the soldiers were rallied after the first volley by the few remaining officers. The little cannon was loaded and fired several times. The Indians shot down the artillerymen and the gun was silenced.

Alligator tells of one little officer who drew his sword and tried to rally his men. He swore at the Indians and was very brave man. This officer must have been Captain Fraser, next in command, as Major Dade was killed by the first volley fired by the Indians.

He gives a full account of what followed, he said the soldiers fought to the last. They took refuge behind trees and exchanged shot for shot. After the firing had continued for a considerable time, the Indians ran out of ammunition and retired for a fresh supply.

An Indian reported to the chiefs that there was a few soldiers left and that they were throwing up a breastwork of logs. The Indians returned with their new supply of ammunition, and fought until the soldiers' ammunition was all gone, and then they were at the mercy of the savages. It is needless to say there was no mercy.

The Indians sent their negro slaves into the improvised fort and found three soldiers alive. They talked to

116

them in English and then clubbed them to death. Alligator said one man was very brave, and refused to surrender. He grabbed an Indian, took his gun away from him and knocked his brains out with one blow of his own gun.

This brave man then ran down the trail until he was pursued by several Indians on horseback and shot down.

Clarke Corroberates Alligator's Story

Daniel F. Clarke, the first man who arrived at Ft. Brooke to tell the tale, corroberates Alligator's story in the main parts. He had received seven wounds, and was only able to get away by pretending to be dead when the Indians and negroes came into the enclosure.

A negro slave gave him a push with his foot and said, "He is dead enough." Clarke remained feigning death until dark. He was as still as his dead comrades who were all around him and several of them partly on him. After nightfall, he crawled out of the bloody pen, and started on his long and painful journey to Fort Brooke, eighty miles away.

The Indians took all the arms and ammunition, so Clarke was unarmed. He fell in with another soldier, who had escaped. They travelled together at night and lay in hiding throughout the day time.

When these two found out the Indians were on their trail, they separated. Soon after they separated Clarke said he heard a volley of shots,

MONUMENT TO DADE'S MEN

and he knew his companion was dead.

Indians Realized the Seriousness Of Their Action

The Indians seemed to realize the fearful slaughter they had made, and their actions following the massacre, seemed to indicate much confusion among them. The Indians' usual custom was to scalp the dead, but few of these soldiers were scalped. They did not take the clothing of the dead soldiers, nor did they rob the dead officers of their jewelry and money.

Alligator said the Indians left the field of massacre hastily, and returned to their base in a swamp. Late that night they were joined by the head chief Osceola, and his band who had murdered General Thompson, the Indian Agent and Lieutenant Smith at Fort King.

Chief Osceola and his men were loaded down with loot from Fort King, and the two bands celebrated their bloody work throughout the remainder of the night. Most of the Indians were drunk on the liquor taken from the Fort.

Osceola brought the scalp of General Thompson. He placed the scalp on a pole and many of the Indians made speeches to the spirit of the departed General.

Bodies of The Soldiers Exposed

For weeks the bodies of the dead soldiers remained exposed to the elements and the prey of vultures. General Edmund P. Gaines landed at Fort Brooke, on Tampa Bay, with a considerable force of men. He marched against the hostile Indians and advanced along the Fort King trail until he came to the scene of the Massacre. He arrived there on February the twentieth, eighteen thirty-six. This was nearly two months after the massacre.

The report was made to the War Department by Captain Ethen Allen Hitchcock, a graduate of West Point, serving as Inspector General of General Gaines command. Captain Hitchcock reports that it was a gruesome sight that greeted the eyes of General Gaines and his men.

The bodies of the dead soldiers were scattered along the trail, each where he had fallen. The dead oxen with their yokes still on their necks were lying where they were shot down. The Indians had evidently not revisited the scene, and no white man was known to have viwed the scene of the massacre until General Gaines and his men arrived.

The dead horses of the dead officers were lying among the men. The ground was littered with boxes and packages that had contained ammunition and supplies.

The small enclosure of logs where the men made their last stand contained the remains of about thirty dead soldiers. The men were lying

TABLET TO THOSE WHO FELL

Appendices

in the position they must have been in when they were killed. Their heads were all toward the breastwork, their arms extended and their bodies parallel to each other, as if they died fighting.

Passing the enclosure they came to a place where other bodies were, showing the position of the men as they marched with the bodies of the officers in front. The bodies of all the officers were identified. Many of the officers and men in General Gaines' command were personal acquaintances and friends of the officers and men who had fallen in the discharge of their duty. General Gaines' command buried the officers in one trench and the men in another. All the usual and proper military honors were paid to the memory of the dead. The remains have since been removed to the National Cemetery at St. Augustine.

The men who lost their lives in the Dade Massacre have a monument in the National Cemetery at St. Augustine, erected by the officers of the Florida Indian Wars. There is another monument on the Campus at West Point Military Academy. And Dade Memorial Park at Bushnell, Florida, marks the spot where the Massacre occurred, and an eighty acre plot of ground owned by the State of Florida is the third and last monument to Major Dade and his fighting men. When General Gaines and his men buried the victims in the long trench, they placed the little six pound cannon at the head of the trench as a fitting monument to these fighting men.

INSIDE THE UNFINISHED FORT

Officers Who Perished

The officers who gave up their lives at the head of their column of patriots were:

Major Francis L. Dade	Lieutenant Basenger
Captain Fraser	Lieutenant Henderson
Captain Gardiner	Lieutenant Mudge
Lieutenant Keais	Dr. J. S. Gatlin, surgeon

The bodies of ninety-eight men, privates and non-commissioned officers, were found and buried. Clarke and two other men finally reached Fort Brook, after suffering great hardships.

Beyond the Battle

THIS TELLS THE STORY

Site of The Battlefield Marked

The battle ground is located inside the corporate limits of Bushnell, Florida, the County seat of Sumter County. With the aid of a sketch copied from a map made by Lieutenant Joseph E. Johnson the exact spot where the massacre occured is definitely located.

Lieutenant Johnson was years later a famous General of the Confederate Army. The Fort King trail is definitely located on maps made of the county in 1848 by the U. S. Geological survey.

To this day you can see the open pine woods, the giant live oaks, the clumps of palmetto, where the Indians hid to murder their victims, and the little lake to the east of the fighting ground.

Resolutions of Respect

The Legislature of the Territory of Florida was in session when the news of the Massacre reached Tallahassee, the Capitol. Suitable resolutions were passed. The flag was placed at half mast and much regret was expressed for the fate of General Dade and his men.

Years later the Legislature of the State of Florida sent a memorial to the United States Congress and requested an appropriation for the purpose of marking the historical spot with a proper monument.

Later the State of Florida appropriated ten thousand dollars to establish the Dade Memorial Park, scenes of which are given in this book.

Dade Monument at West Point

There is a monument in front of Memorial Hall, at West Point Military Academy erected in memory of Major Dade and his command of one hundred and eight men. This monument was moved to its present site several years ago. It was erected on the West Point grounds in eighteen forty-five.

The original report of Captain E. A. Hitchcock is published on page 289 of "History of West Point"

Appendices

A DRIVE IN DADE MEMORIAL PARK

published in 1864, by Captain Edward C. Boynton, adjutant of the Military Academy at the time of publication.

This report was dated Fort King, Florida, February the twenty-second, eighteen thirty-six.

Roster of The Men Who Were Killed

These are the men who were massacred on December the twenty-eighth, eighteen thirty-five:

Second Regiment Artillery

Belton, Edward
Black, William
Bourke, Richard
Barton, Rufus
Bogen, Owen
Bowen, Richard
Brandon, Henry
Cooper, Philip, *Sergeant*
Clark, Nicholas, *Corporal*
Carney, William, *Musician*
Craig, Joseph
De Courtney, Edward
Dunlap, James, *Corporal*
Davis, Thomas
Gibson, Robert
Grant, Isaac
Gillett, Alphens
Hood, John, *Sergeant*
Hicks, Charles T., *Musician*
Howard, George, *Artificer*
Halter, John
Keiss, John
Loughlin, Anthony
Lyon, John
McCarty, John M.
McDonald, James
Malcolm, Robert
McMee, Hugh
McGene, Wm., *Artificer*
Notley, William
Perry, Hugh
Patton, John A.
Phillips, Reuben
Rooney, Patrick
Ryan, Michael, *Corporal*
Robertson, William
Rafferty, Patrick
Reilley, John
Sayin, Thomas
Schneider, Casper
Taylor, William
Taylor, Isaac

Hurley, John
Holmes, William
Hill, Cornelius
Jewell, Aaron
Kenny, Michael
Knott, Thomas

Taylor, Hiram
Thorton, Thomas
Wilson, Joseph
Wormater, Orville
Wright, William
Wiggins, John M.

Third Regiment Artillery

Bertram, George
Chapman, Benjamin, *Sergeant*
Cannakey, Patrick
Carpenter, R. C.
Dodge, Samuel R.
Farley, A. C. W., *Sergeant*
Flannigan, William
Felix, John C.
Haberyish, George
Hall, Jordan
Kimberly, Samuel
Lombey, Jacob
Lemon, Samuel
Minton, William
Monroe, Donald
Mainahan, John
Schaffer, John
Session, Henry
Tuck, Washington
Violinie, John, *Sergeant*
Vreeland, Richard
Wells, Philander, *Corporal*
Wagner, Henry, *Artificer*
Wright, Samuel S.
Williams, John
Webb, Sylvester
Wenkins, Daniel
Young, Geo. C., *Corporal*
York, George
Jones, Alexander

Fourth Regiment Infantry

Barnes, John
Campbell, Donald
Cunningham, Michael
Douglass, John
Donovan, Cornel
Downey, William
Nates, Enoch
Hall, Samuel
Jones, Wiley
Mackhum, John

Documents Found In Dade Monument

There are a number of interesting documents in the Dade Monument at West Point. There are several original maps, showing the location of the Massacre, a complete roll of

Major Dade's men, showing the home addresses of each soldier killed, also a document giving a short sketch of the massacre with drawings showing the position of the men as they fell.

Memorial in Dade Monument

This document is deposited in the Dade Monument at West Point Military Academy:

"This monument is Erected by the officers and men of the second and third Regiments of Artillery, and fourth Regiment of infantry, and by the Medical Staff, in memory of their Comrades who fell in battle with the Seminole Indians of Florida, on December twenty-eighth, eighteen thirty five.

The Detachment left Fort Brooke, Tampa Bay, for Fort King Florida (distant one hundred and one miles) the twenty-third of December. The force was small—one hundred and seven men and one six pounder—The road abounding in thickets, hammocks and places of concealment and the Indians—(numbering about fourteen hundred warriors) warlike, well armed and had declared that they would allow no armed body to pass through their country without attempting to destroy it.

Fully aware of the danger of the march, and expecting a severe conflict, though with the hope that a *portion* of the command would get through, this little band started, in obedience to orders issued by those who knew not so well the strength

LIEUTENANT MUDGE FELL HERE

and disposition of the enemy.

The writer of this accompanied the detachment to their first encampment, and received directions from two of the officers to settle up their affairs in case they did not survive. Thus forewarned and on their guard, they advanced into the country.

On the morning of the fifth day—December the twenty eighth, at about eight o'clock, when the command had marched some four miles from its last encampment—seven miles north of the Withlacoochee, and was about sixty five miles north by east of Fort Brooke, the Seminoles opened a murderous fire from the Palmetto thickets and bushes.

Appendices

SCENE IN DADE PARK

Major Dade, the Commander, with the advance guard, two hundred yards in front of the main body, Captain Fraser and the leading files of the main body all fell during the first fire.

Part of the detachment then extended, the six pounder field piece was brought into action, and after a contest of more than two hours, the Indians retired, leaving but thirty odd of Dade's Command still alive.

The survivors, many of them wounded, felled some trees, and were forming a small triangular breastwork, when the Indians, who had been withdrawn, by their Chief, *Jumper*, and were told by him that they had killed enough for one day, received a large accession to their force, under *Alligator* who assumed command, renewed the conflict, (about eleven A. M.) and in a little while, all our men were killed or disabled.

Two private soldiers escaped during the first engagement, and reached Tampa on the 29th and 30th (Thomas and Sprague, of B Company, Third Artillery). Two others, Ranson Clark and Edward De Courcey, who were shockingly wounded, and left on the ground as dead by the Indians, started to return the next morning. They were discovered and pursued by a mounted Indian, and separating for safety, De Courcey was overtaken and Clarke escaped, and on the afternoon of the 31st reached Tampa Bay.

Clark recovered, and gave a very connected account of the Conflict, and its termination.

The Ground was not visited by any one until the 20th of February following, when the bodies were found as they had fallen.

This event, succeeding a peace of thirty years, created a strong excitement throughout the land, and large bodies of Volunteers marched into Florida to punish the Seminoles. Seven years of War, with a great expenditure of life and treasure, followed and as the Indians surrendered, or were caught they were removed to the Arkansas.

Peace was made in 1842 and about 100 warriors, with their families, yet remained in Florida—South of Peas

123

Beyond the Battle

BAND STAND IN DADE PARK

Creek—(Tatuhk-Chopks Hatchee) at this day,—May 1845."

A list of the dead accompanies this sheet, and a Sketch of the Battleground is hereon drawn.

The Story of Dade Park

This story is taken from information contained in a folder written by Judge J. C. B. Koonce, of Taveres, Florida. I would like to print the folder in full, the Judge writes it in beautiful language, much better than I can tell it, but the lack of space forbids.

Three Massacres in America

The Dade Massacre in 1835, was the first of three disasters to American soldiers that stand out in American History. In this battle Major Dade's entire command was anhilated with the exception of three men. In retaliation of this surprise after thirty years of peace, The Seminole War was fought for seven years.

The Fall of the Alamo, in March 1836 where practically all of a command of 140 men were massacred by four thousand Mexicans, less than three months after the Dade Massacre, was the second.

The third was the massacre of General Custer with two hundred and eight men on the Little Big Horn in 1876.

The history of the Dade Massacre has been practically unknown outside of army circles and in the State of Florida, where we hear of Dade City and Dade County and Fort Bassenger.

The Fall of the Alamo is known and the fame of Bowie, Crockett, and the rest of Travis' men is told wherever the English tongue is spoken.

The last stand of General Custer and his command before hordes of Souix warriors under Sitting Bull is known to the last detail by every school boy and girl.

It is high time that somebody was telling the world of the brave stand and the supreme sacrifice of Brevet Major F. L. Dade and his little band of one hundred and ten patriots.

Appendices

State of Florida Marks the Spot

More than eighty-five years this important battle field remained unmarked and unnoticed. In 1921 the State of Florida through its Legislature made an appropriation to purchase eighty acres of land surrounding the battle field. This land has been converted into Dade Memorial Park. There was another appropriation in 1923 to further improve this beauty spot in Florida.

Governor Hardee appointed Judge J. C. B. Koonce, of Tavares, Judge F. C. Cubberly, of Gainesville and Mrs. A. M. Roland of Bushnell as Commissioners to carry out the provisions of the act of the legislature. How well they used the appropriation and how beautiful they made this naturally beautiful park will be noted at a glance at Dade Park.

But these Commissioners who have done so well, must have an annual appropriation to keep this beautiful park up to the standard to which it was established. If this little book can in a wee might help to get the proper recognition of Dade Park, and even a modest support for maintenance of this memorial, I will feel well paid for the effort of issuing it.

This Park is well worth a visit to Sumter County and to Bushnell to see it. The Park is now in the city limits of Bushnell.

Dade Park Cannot Be Described

Dade Park cannot be described. It must be seen and felt. Drive over a fine asphalt street from the Court House in Bushnell, down the Plaza, main street and Seminole drive past giant Live Oak trees festooned with Spanish Moss to the Gateway of Dade Park.

There is a small picket fence that marks the Fort King Trail. Numerous monuments showing the exact spot where Major Dade fell and similar monuments marking the places where the other officers breathed their last. A replica of the little log breastworks that were in course of erection where the last of the men were killed, a monument with a life sized soldier done in bronze, and tablets giving the name of each man that played his part in this tragedy. Then we have a beautiful and well appointed recreation hall called Tustenugge, which means War Chief.

Rock bridges over the little streams, the band stand, the picnic ground where every Fourth of July the memory of Major Dade and his Command is told in oratory and song to celebrate the freedom that these brave soldiers helped to create. The people from surrounding counties and some from other States congregate here to view the battle ground and hear again and again of the deeds of valor.

What Shall We Do With It

Many people have suggested that we give Dade Park to the Government to convert into a National Park. Others say "It was Florida's war and it is Florida's park, let the State keep it." Everyone seems to want to help, all they need is someone to tell them what to do.

There is one thing certain. Dade Park is too important, too historical and too beautiful to be neglected. There must be a fund for maintainance from somewhere.

The State has done well in establishing this Memorial. The State will do more and maintain it as it should be maintained, if the people will only get behind the movement and urge it.

The Commissioners have done well with the means at hand. Nobody could do more and few there are who could do as well. They need the people of the State of Florida behind them, they need the patriotic people of the United States behind them.

I have correspondance with U. S. Senator Duncan U. Fletcher, Judge Cubberly and Judge Koonce. They are all willing to do more for Dade Park, although they have all shown their interest and devotion to this Memorial Park.

Senator Fletcher says he is ready to give his services, if it is desired to make the site of the Dade Massacre declared a National Monument.

Judge Koonce says for the present he prefers it to be a State Park. Personally I would like to help either course that the Commissioners decide to persue. Anyway I want to stir up interest in the Park, so something will be done for the up keep of this splendid Memorial.

Every American who visits Florida should visit this spot, which is hallowed by the supreme sacrifice made by true Americans in their effort to help build up the wonderful State of Florida.

Appendices

Appendix C

Dates of the Dade Annual Commemorative Events

Dec. 28, 1980

~~Dec. 27, 1981~~ **(Rescheduled to 2/14/82)**

Jan. 1 + 2, 1983

Jan. 14, 1984

Dec. 29, 1984 **(small skirmish)**

Dec. 28, 1985 **(1st full battle)**

Dec. 27, 1986

Jan. 2 + 3, 1988 **(Sat. skirmish, Sun. full battle)**

Dec. 31, 1988 + Jan. 1, 1989

Dec. 30 + 31, 1989 **(1st Full battle <u>both</u> days)**

Dec. 29 + 30, 1990

Dec. 28 + 29, 1991

Jan. 2 + 3, 1993

Jan. 1 + 2, 1994 **(2nd day cancelled)**

Dec. 31, 1994 + Jan. 1, 1995

Dec. 30 + 31, 1995

Dec. 28 + 29, 1996

Jan. 3 + 4, 1998

Jan. 2 + 3, 1999

Jan. 1 +2, 2000

Dec. 30 + 31, 2000

Dec. 29 + 30, 2001

Dec. 28 + 29, 2002

~~Jan. 2 + 3, 2004~~ **(rained out)**

Jan. 1 + 2, 2005

Dec. 31, 2005 + Jan. 1, 2006

Dec. 30 + 31, 2006

Dec. 29 + 30, 2007

Jan. 3 + 4, 2009

Jan. 2 + 3, 2010

Jan. 1 + 2, 2011

Jan. 7 + 8, 2012

Jan. 5 + 6, 2013

Jan. 4 + 5, 2014

Jan. 3 + 4, 2015

Jan. 2, 2016 **(2nd day cancelled)**

Jan. 7 + 8, 2017

Jan. 6 + 7, 2018

Jan. 5 + 6, 2019

Jan. 4 + 5, 2020

~~Jan. 2 + 3, 2021~~ **(Covid-19)**

Jan. 1 + 2, 2022

Jan. 7 + 8, 2023

Appendix D

SUPERVISORS OF THE DADE BATTLEFIELD PROPERTY

Dade Memorial Park
Dade Battlefield State Historic Site
Dade Battlefield Historic State Park

Caretakers   Superintendents   Managers
(Titles changed along with the status of the park.)

Enos Hunt	1921 - 1925
Isaac D. "Ike" Hogans	1925 - 1938
Vernon C. Huff	1938 - 1943
Edwin Woodard	1943 - 1951
Arthur Clark	1952 - 1961
John Hale	1961 - Sep. 1964
G. C. Tiller	Sep. 1964 - 1975
Carl Parks	1975 - 1978
Dal Myers	1978 - 1979
Wayne Edwards	1979 - Mar. 1989
Jeff Montgomery	Apr. 1989 – 1993
Jeff DiMaggio	1994 – Jun. 1997
Barbara Roberts	Jul. 1997 – Mar. 2004
Tracey Standridge	May 2004 – Mar. 2009
Bob Baker	Apr. 2009 – May 2010
Bruce Whiting	Jun. 2010 – Jun. 2013
Bill Gruber	Oct. 2013 -

Appendix E

Dade Battlefield Society
Chartered June 8, 1987

Presidents

Virginia Bell	Jun. 1987 - Jan. 1989
Sheila Mann	Feb. – Dec. 1989
Jackson Walker	Jan. – Dec. 1990
Sheila Mann	Jan. 1991 – Jul. 1996
Frank Laumer	Aug. 1996 – Feb. 1998
Jerry Morris	Mar. 1998 – Jun. 1999
Nell Kreis	Jul. 1999 – Jun. 2001
John DeLancett	Jul. 2001 – Jun. 2003
Jean McNary	Jul. 2003 – Jun. 2009
Steven Rinck	Jul. 2009 – Jun. 2014
Paul Remis	Jul. 2014 – Jun. 2018
Steven Rinck	Jul. 2018 – Jun. 2019
Karen Cloud	Jul. 2019 – Jun. 2020
Ross Lamoreaux	Jul. 2020 – Jun. 2022
Amber Lamoreaux	Jul. 2022 -

Image Credits for Figures 1-52

1. Ellis, Edward Sylvester. *The Indian wars of the United States, from the first settlement at Jamestown, in 1607 to the close of the great uprising of 1890-91*. P. D. Farrell & Co., Grand Rapids, Michigan, 1892.
2. Accessed at Wikipedia September 29, 2021.
3. Sumter County Historical Society vertical files, folder BU-P0020, March 18, 2014.
4. *The spot where General Dade was massacred in the Seminole War.* 1911 (circa). State Archives of Florida, Florida Memory. <https://www.floridamemory.com/items/show/161109>, accessed 21 August 2021.
5. Accessed at Wikipedia September 29, 2021.
6. Sumter County Historical Society.
7. Dade Battlefield Historic State Park files.
8. Photo by Author.
9. Sumter County Historical Society.
10. Harmon, William Z., 1916-1974. *Monument to Major Francis Dade's command at Dade Battlefield Historic State Park - Bushnell, Florida.* 1940 (circa). State Archives of Florida, Florida Memory. <https://www.floridamemory.com/items/show/41328>, accessed 21 August 2021.
11. Smithsonian American Art Museum.
12. Tourist booklet, Frank Laumer Collection.
13. Sumter County Historical Society.
14. Sumter County Historical Society.
15. Photo by Author, July 8, 2022.
16. *The YMCA and World War I*. University of Minnesota Libraries, Minneapolis, MN, Libguides.umn.edu, accessed October 2, 2021.
17. Photo by Author.
18. Collection of the U.S. House of Representatives.
19. Sumter County Historical Society.
20. Florida Historical Society.

21. Courtesy of Liz Sumner.
22. Courtesy of Liz Sumner.
23. Sumter County Past.
24. Dade Battlefield Historic State Park files.
25. Courtesy Edwin Force.
26. Courtesy Edwin Force.
27. Courtesy Inez McMilland.
28. Courtesy Inez McMilland.
29. Courtesy Edwin Force.
30. Courtesy Marsha Perkins.
31. Schaeffer, Charles H., d. 1959. *Lodge at Dade Battlefield Historic State Park - Bushnell, Florida.* 1956. State Archives of Florida, Florida Memory. <https://www.floridamemory.com/items/show/116527>, accessed 21 August 2021.
32. Holland, Karl E., 1919-1993. *Visitors at museum at the Dade Battlefield Historic State Park - Bushnell, Florida*. 1976. State Archives of Florida, Florida Memory. <https://www.floridamemory.com/items/show/59108>, accessed 21 August 2021.
33. Photo by Author.
34. Harmon, William Z., 1916-1974. *Gatling gun and replica of log fort at the Dade Battlefield Historic State Park - Bushnell, Florida.* 1940 (circa). State Archives of Florida, Florida Memory. <https://www.floridamemory.com/items/show/41330>, accessed 21 August 2021.
35. Sumter County Historical Society.
36. Frank Laumer Collection.
37. Seminole Wars Foundation Archives.
38. Courtesy Andrew Foster.
39. Courtesy Andrew Foster.
40. Courtesy Heather Burney.
41. Courtesy Heather Burney.
42. Courtesy Don Dickey.
43. Courtesy Joe Carrier.

Image Credits

44. Courtesy Florida National Guard Command Historian.
45. Dade Battlefield Historic State Park files.
46. Dade Battlefield Historic State Park files.
47. Dade Battlefield Historic State Park files.
48. Courtesy Myrna Erler-Bradshaw.
49. Courtesy Marsha Perkins.
50. Florida Historical Society.
51. League, Susan L. "Gayle Hunt: An Unsung Hero of Sumter County." *Sumter News-Sun,* November 10, 2021.
52. Courtesy Sam Coverston.

Endnotes

Introduction
1. "Dade's Breakfast Pond." *Tampa Times*. Tampa, Florida. April 24, 1929, p.10.

Chapter 1: The Destiny
1. Laumer, Frank. "Dade's Last Command." University Press of Florida, Gainesville, 1995, 47, 177; Morris, Jerry C. and Hough, Jeffrey A. "The Fort King Road, Then and Now." Seminole Wars Foundation, Inc., Dade City, Florida, 2009, xi.
2. Coe, Charles H. "Red Patriots: The Story of The Seminoles." The Editor Publishing Company, Cincinnati, 1895, 63; Mahon, John K. "History of The Second Seminole War 1835/1842, Revised Edition." University Press of Florida, Gainesville, 1985, 146; Laumer, Frank. "Massacre!" University of Florida Press, Gainesville, 1968, 164; "Dade Battlefield Historic State Park Approved Unit Management Plan". State of Florida Department of Environmental Protection, Division of Recreation and Parks, Tallahassee, Florida, October 2017, 31.
3. Morris, op. cit.,xii; *Population Schedules of the Sixth Census of the United States, Florida,* 1840.
4. Otto, John Solomon. "Hillsborough County (1850): A Community in the South Florida Flatwoods." The Florida Historical Quarterly, Florida Historical Society, Vol. 62, No. 2, October 1983, 183-184.
5. "Registration Papers for Thomas R. Pierce House," Bushnell, Florida, National Register of Historic Places, NRIS #96000022; Nisbet, Newton A., ed. "Early History of Florida and of Sumter County." *Collection of the George Nichols Public Library,* Wildwood, Florida, 1969.
6. Sumter County Historical Society website: http://www.rootsweb.ancestry.com/fischs/; Parish, Samuel: "Sumter County-A Chronicle of Change in Settlement and Residential Growth." Florida Humanities Council, date unknown, 2; Elfers, C.A. "Salute to Sumpter County, The Imperial Valley of Florida." Federal Writers Project, Sumter County Writers Program, 1938; "City of Bushnell First Settled in Year 1853." Sumter County Times, Bushnell, Florida, February 23, 1956, 74; Barthoff, J. F. and Bogess, F. C. M. "South Florida, The Italy of America-Its Climate, Soil and Productions." Ashmead Brothers, Jacksonville, Florida, 1881, 20.
7. Nisbet, *Op. cit.*
8. Sumter County, Florida Public Records: Vol. T/p. 3; Vol. 27/p. 44.
9. *Army and Navy Chronicle,* Vol.3, No. 10, September 8, 1836; Military Secretary of the War Department, in a letter to Stephen Sparkman,

Endnotes

January 20, 1905; "Sparkman's Activity," The Ocala Evening Star, Ocala, Florida, December 19, 1907, 1; H.R. 6093, 62nd Congress, April 19, 1911; H.R. 5771, 64th Congress, December 15, 1915; Secretary of War ad interim, in a letter to the Chairman, Committee on the Library, House of Representatives, February 28, 1916.

10. Herbert J. Drane, in a letter to Colonel H. L. Landers, February 10, 1930. Florida Historical Society, Cocoa, Florida.
11. Starnes, C. L., Feature story on Judge Koonce, title unknown, date unknown, Founder's Day Edition, *The Wildwood Herald Express*, The George Nichols Public Library Collection, now in the archives of The Sumter County Historical Society, Bushnell, Florida; Jean McNary, conversation with the author, Dade City Florida, June 22, 2015.

Chapter 2: The Recovery

1. Powers, Ormund. "Unusual Interest From A Local Judge Kept Dade Battlefield Park Alive". *Orlando Sentinel.* June 1, 1994, 4. Access: http://articles.orlandosentinel.com/1994-06-01/news/9406010_1_koonce-dade-battlefield-judge.
2. Roberts, Albert Hubbard. "The Dade Massacre." Florida Historical Society Quarterly, vol. 5, no. 3, Pepper Printing Company, Gainesville, Florida, January, 1927, 125.
3. News item. *The Ocala Evening Star,* Ocala, Florida, October 4, 1898, 4; "Koonce to Address Jaycees on Monday." *The Orlando Sentinel,* Orlando, Florida, January 15, 1933, 8.
4. "County Courthouse." Sumter County Website, www.sumtercountyfl.gov, accessed April 29, 2021; "A Big Deal." *Sumter County Times,* March 12, 1909; "Looking Back Sumter County – A Photographic Essay". Compiled by Doris Valentine. Sponsored by The Sumter County Historical Society. Sundial Print Shop, Bushnell, Florida, 1981, 14; Sumter County Public Records: Vol 66/203.
5. Levon Williams, interview by author, Bushnell, Florida, August 31, 2013; "Fletcher is On Tour of Southern Florida." "The Florida Senator took hard line on bad bankers during the Depression." *St. Petersburg Times,* March 21, 2009; *The Tampa Tribune,* May 18, 1914, 5; Florida Office of Secretary of State. J.C.B. Koonce. March 31, 1914. State Archives of Florida, Florida Memory. <htps://www.floridamemory.com/items/show/309029>, accessed August 22, 2021.
6. Herbert J. Drane, in a letter to Benjamin Harrison, August 30, 1917. Florida Historical Society, Cocoa, Florida; Laws of Florida, House Resolution No. 20, Tallahassee, Florida, 1917, p. 338; Herbert J. Drane, in a letter to Mrs. William Hines, July 5, 1919. Florida Historical Society, Cocoa, Florida.

7. Cubberly, Frederick. "The Dade Massacre." Government Printing Office, Washington, D.C.; Journal of the House of Representatives of the State of Florida of the Session of 1921, April 11, 1921, 231 and April 14, 1921, 312; Trice, John C. "Bill For Monument Marking Site Dade Massacre Is Passed." *The Tampa Tribune*, May 6, 1921, 4; "Dade Massacre Memorial Sure." *The Tampa Morning Tribune*, May 10, 1921, 4.
8. Herbert J. Drane, in a letter to J.C.B. Koonce, April 16, 1921. Florida Historical Society, Cocoa, Florida.
9. Laws of Florida, Chapter 8503, Tallahassee, Florida, 1921; Valentine, Doris, ed. "Looking Back Sumter County – A Photographic Essay." The Sumter County Historical Society, Bushnell, Florida, 1981; "Anniversary Celebration Is Announced." *The Tampa Times*, June 24, 1921.
10. Freeman, Gilbert. "Massacre of Dade And His Command Is Commemorated." *The Tampa Tribune*, July 8, 1921, 1&4; *The Tampa Tribune*, July 9, 1921, 11; "Bushnell To Act as Host to Picnickers." *The Tampa Times*, July 6, 1921, 12; "Sumter to Bond for Additional Roadways." *The Tampa Tribune*. July 13, 1922, 3; "Apprpriations-Dade Memorial Park." State of Florida Official Communications, River Buford, Attorney General, to Ernest Amos, State Comptroller. Tallahassee, Florida, September 21, 1921, 130-131.
11. Washington, Ray. "A Battle Stirs Behind Dade Statue." *Gainesville Sun,* Gainesville, Florida, September 12, 1983; Sam Coverston, interview by author, Bushnell, Florida, October 10. 2014; Personal observations by author, Bushnell, Florida, May 21, 2014; Winnie Murphy, in a letter to Jim Tilford, January 29, 1983. Dade Battlefield Historic State Park Archives, Bushnell, Florida.
12. "Bushnell Pleased Over Celebration." *The Tampa Tribune,* July 9, 1921; "Dade Memorial Park Formally Dedicated." *The Tampa Tribune,* July 5, 1922.
13. Gayle Hunt, interview by author, Bushnell, Florida, November 4, 2014; Scrammy Hunt, interview by Karen Cloud, Dade Battlefield Historic State Park, 2018; Coverston, *Op. cit.*; Adams, Jamie. "Marsh Remembers Bygone Days at Dade Park." Sumter County Times, Bushnell, Florida, February 18, 1999; Frank Hamilton, interview by author, Bushnell, Florida, October 15, 2013; Howell, Jr., P. B. "Piney Woods, Swamp Water and Gator Tales." Lifestyles Press, Tavares, Florida, 1998, 23 & 24; Adams, Jamie. "Some recollections about Dade Park." *The Sumter County Times,* February 2, 1999; "Sumter County Women Hold Meeting on Site of Historic Interest." *The Tampa Tribune,* March 3, 1924, 9; Koonce, J.C.B. "Dade Massacre and Dade Park." Pamphlet, Dade Battlefield Historic State Park Archives, Bushnell, Florida, 1935.

Endnotes

14. Wysong, Elsie Baylor, ed. "History of Sumter County, Florida." Self-published, 1993.
15. Letters between J.C.B. Koonce and Herbert Drane, August 17 & 25, and September 6, 1922. Florida Historical Society, Cocoa, Florida; Josephine Strong-Simmons, interview by author, Bushnell, Florida, May 26, 2017; Koonce, *Op. cit.*
16. Journal of the House of Representatives (Florida), April 8, 1935, 33-34; "Woman's Club Hears Judge Koonce". *The Orlando Sentinel,* November 9, 1934, 8; News item. *The Tampa Tribune,* December 12, 1935, 18; "Indian Peace". *The Orlando Sentinel,* April 28, 1935, 10.
17. "Florida Centennial To Be In December." *The Miami Herald,* November 25, 1935, 16. "Widow of Slain Major Dade Lived in Pensacola.: *Pensacola News Journal,* December 28, 1935, 1; "Five Thousand Attend Service Memorializing Major Dade at Bushnell." *Punta Gorda Herald,* January 1, 1936, 1&8; "Dade Massacre Centennial To Be Held Dec. 28." *The Tampa Tribune, December 12, 1935, 18;* "Dade Memorial Attracts 2,000." *The Sunday Sentinel Star,* Orlando, Florida, December 29, 1935, 1-2; John W. Outlaw, interview by author, Inverness, Florida, October 5, 2013; "Florida State Park History." *Florida Park Service Ranger Association.* Accessed November 22, 2021 at website: http://fpsra.org.

Chapter 3: The Koonce Show

1. Hamilton, Belle. "Judge Koonce Dade Park Work Praised". *The Orlando Sentinel,* June 14, 1934, 1.
2. Ancestry.com, accessed February 14, 2022.
3. "Whig and American Meeting in Jones County". *American Advocate (Kinston, NC),* May 7, 1857, 2; "Jones County Democratic Convention". *Kinston Journal (NC),* October 14, 1880, 3.
4. "Closing Exercises of Kinsey's School". *Kinston (NC) Journal,* June 10, 1880, 2; Walker, D. R. "Closing Exercises of LaGrange Institute". *New Berne (NC) Weekly Journal,* June 8, 1882, 4; Starnes, C. l. Feature story on Judge Koonce (untitled, undated), Founders' Day Edition, *The Wildwood Herald Express,* The George Nichols Public Library Collection, now in the archves of The Sumter County Historical Society, Bushnell, Florida; Vickers-Smith, Lillian D. "Judge Mixes Law And Moulding". *The Tampa Tribune,* March 10, 1940, 46; "LaGrange Items". *The Daily Journal,* New Berne (NC), July 10, 1884, 1; "A North Carolinian in Florida". *The Daily Journal,* April 13, 1895, 1; "A Romantic Marriage". *New Berne Daily Journal,* September 4, 1895, 1; Koonce, J.C.B. "To The Public". *Sumter County Times,* July 28, 1905, 2.
5. Journal of The House of Representatives (Florida), April 7, May 2, 29, June 1, 1899, May 22, 1901, May 5, 8, 1903.
6. "Press Compliments". *Sumter County Times,* April 29, 1904, 4.

7. "Judge Tillman Dies in Tampa". *The Tampa Tribune*, March 1, 1910, 16; "A Good Appointment". *The Ocala Evening Star*, March 12, 1910, 2; United States Census, Precinct 1, Marion County, Florida. Enumerated April 16, 1910.
8. *The Ocala Evening Star*, June 23, 1915, 4, September 4, 1918, 4, February 23, 1919, 3; James C. B. Koonce, United States of America Passport, November 8, 1918.
9. *The Ocala Evening Star*, February 1, 1919, 3; "The YMCA and World War I". University of Minnesota Libraries, Minneapolis, Minnesota. Accessed at Libguides.uma.edu on October 2, 2021; "Summary of World War Work of the American YMCA". The International Committee of Young Men's Christian Associations, 1920, 114, 119, 120, 124.
10. United States Census, Precinct 8, Bushnell, Florida. Enumerated January 3, 1920; "Judge Koonce Will Locate in Leesburg". *The Tampa Tribune*, February 26, 1921, 3; Journal of The House of Representatives (Florida), April 11, 1921.
11. "Bronze Tablet Erected To Honor Judge Koonce". *The Tampa Tribune*, September 10, 1922, 2.
12. "Koonce Judge Futch Attrny". *Tallahassee Democrat*, June 12, 1923, 2; "Judge Koonce". *The Tampa Tribune*, June 26, 1923, 8; "Civil Docket Delay Is Seen". *The Saint Petersburg Times*, February 4, 1927, 6; "Circuit Judge Koonce Releases Final Group of Bank Defendents". *Orlando Evening Star*, July 22, 1930, 1; Morgan, Philip. "Sumter Countians Ambush State On Bicentennial Trail." *Tampa Tribune,* February 15, 1976, 9; "Bar Banquet at Wyoming". *Orlando Evening Star*, April 12, 1930, 5; "Sumter County Women Hold Meeting on Site Of Historic Interest". *The Tampa Tribune*, March 3, 1924, 9; "Koonce to Address Jaycees on Monday". *Orlando Sentinel*, January 15, 1933, 8; "Leesburg, Ocala D. A. R. Plan Visit To Memorial Park". *The Tampa Tribune*, January 27, 1935, 29; "Judge Koonce To Dedicate New Statue of Osceola". *The Tampa Tribune*, January 26, 1939, 7; "Judge Speaks Before Rotary". *Orlando Evening Star*, August 7, 1940, 3; *The Rotarian*, February, 1948; "J.C.B. Koonce, Veteran Judge, Dies At Eustis". *The Tampa Tribune*, September 16, 1948, 2.
13. McCall, Maud B. "Sumter County", a student essay, 1923. Florida Heritage Collection, State University of Florida, http://palmm.digital.flvc.org/islandora/object/palmm/o3Aroot; Gayle Hunt, interview by author, Bushnell, Florida, November 4, 2014; Howell, Jr., P.B. "Piney Woods, Swamp Water and Gator Tales". Lifestyle Press, Tavares, Florida, 1998, 25&26; "Bar Banquet...", Op.cit; "Judge Speaks...", Op.cit.
14. Vickers-Smith, Op.cit; Powers, Ormund "Unusual interest from a local judge kept Dade Battlefield park alive". *The Orlando Sentinel*, June

Endnotes

1, 1994, 4; Rencher, Wm. O. "Central Florida". *The Orlando Sentinel*, August 15, 1931, 4; "Rin Tin Tin At Eustis". *Orlando Evening Star*, February 23, 1933, 5; Howell, Jr., P.B., Op.cit.

15. "Veteran Jurist Dies". *The Palm Beach Post*, September 16, 1948, 5; "J.C.B. Koonce, Veteran Judge, Dies At Eustis". *The Tampa Tribune*, September 16, 1948, 2; Reed, Rick. "Piece of history found." *Daily Commercial*, Leesburg, Florida, November 29, 2001.
16. Obituary for Herbert Drane. *Lakeland Ledger and Star-Telegram*. Thursday Evening, August 12, 1947; "Drane Recalls Introduction to Henry B. Plant". *The Tampa Times*. September 5, 1932, 2.
17. Plummer, Herbert. "Washington Daybook". *Orlando Evening Star*. November 9, 1929, 2; "H. J. Drane on Visit to Seminoles". *The Tampa Times*. November 2, 1931, 8.
18. "A Forgotten Massacre". *The Greenfield Vedette*. Greenfield, Missouri, July 7, 1921, 6; Arthur Williams to Herbert Drane. The Florida Historical Society, Jacksonville, Florida, March 6, 1930.
19. J.C.B. Koonce to Herbert Drane, March 3, 1930, and Herbert Drane to J.C.B. Koonce, February 21, 1930. Drane, H. J. Papers 1917-1944. The Florida Historical Society, Cocoa, Florida.
20. "Drane, Former Congressman, Hurt in Fall". *The Tampa Tribune*. July 18, 1946; "Drane, Former Congressman, Dies at 84". *Tampa Morning Tribune*. August 12, 1947; Obituary, op. cit.
21. U.S. Census Records accessed at Ancestry.com on October 21, 2021; *The Tampa Tribune*, September 22, 1929, 24; *The Tampa Tribune*, November 11, 1929, 20; J.C.B. Koonce to Herbert Drane, August 17, 1922; *The Miami News*, September 3, 1937, 2.
22. U.S. Census Records accessed at Ancestry.com on October 18, 2021; Lutts, Ralph H. "Frederick C. Cubberly: 'A Friend of the Oppressed'." *The Florida Historical Quarterly*. Fall 2017, vol. 96, no. 2, 201, 203-204, 215-216.
23. "Cubberly Sworn In As U.S. Attorney." *The Miami News*. December 17, 1921, 25; Lutts, Op. cit., 217, 229-231; "Threatening Letter Signed K.K.K. Received By Federal Attorneys Here." *Pensacola News Journal*. May 8, 1924, 1; Cubberly Family data from Ancestry.com, accessed on Februrary 24, 2022; "Fred Cubberly Death's Victim". *Tallahassee Democrat*. August 12, 1932, 7.
24. History of Florida Past and Present, Historical and Biographical. The Lewis Publishing Company, Chicago and New York, 1923 vol. III, 169-170; Social notation on R.F. Collins. *The Sumter County Times*. Sumterville, Florida, April 15, 1904, 1.
25. Advertising appearing in *The Sumter County Times*, June 2, 1905, 3, June 7, 1907, 4, and March 12, 1909, 4; History of Florida, Op.cit.; "Executive Appointments". *The Weekly Tribune (Tampa)*, January 30, 1908.

26. "City of Bushnell First Settled in Year 1853". *Sumter County Times.* Bushnell, Florida, February 23, 1956; History of Florida, Op.cit.; Sumter County, Florida Public Records: Vol. 74/p. 375, Vol. H/p. 506, Vol. 83/pp. 492, 494.
27. Valentine, Doris, ed. "Looking Back Sumter County – A Photographic Essay." The Sumter County Historical Society, Bushnell, Florida, 1981; "Identified Local Banking Panics." www.semanticscholar.org, accessed April 25, 2022; Marsha Woodard Perkins, interview by author, Bushnell, Florida, March 11, 2021; Sam Coverston, interview by author, Bushnell, Florida, October 10, 2014; U.S. Census records of 1920, 1930, and 1940, Eustis, Florida City Directory of 1926, Florida State Census of 1935, accessed at Ancestry.com on October 21, 2021; "Deaths And Funeral Notices." *Orlando Evening Star.* August 4, 1959, 10.

Chapter 4: The Second Dade Massacre

1. *Pensacola News Journal*, May 14, 1937, 7; "House Passes Salary Boost." *Tampa Times,* May 27, 1937, 16; "Parks, Forests and Memorials." *Tallahassee Democrat,* July 29, 1939, 9; "$7,500 Appropriation Approved To Build Dade Memorial park." *Tampa Tribune,* May 16, 1939; "Recreation." *Tallahassee Democrat*, August 25, 1939, 7; "State Cabinet Holds Up Fund For Memorial." *Tampa Tribune*, March 24, 1938; "State Only Able to Pay Most Bills.", February 22, 1939; 600 Annually Voted for Dade Memorial Park. "$600 Annually Voted for Dade Memorial Park." *Tampa Tribune*, May 28, 1941, 6; "Other Budgets Cut." *Tampa Tribune",* July 29, 1942, 14; "Beville Family Meets at Park". *Tampa Tribune*, August 8, 1937, 26; "Beville Kin Reunion Planned in Bushnell", *Tampa Times*, July 12, 1938; "Beville Family has Reunion at Bushnell". *Tampa Tribune,* July 14, 1940; "Bushnell Observes Fourth at Dade Park." *Orlando Evening Star,* July 6, 1937, 10; "3000 at Bushnell Homecoming Fete." *Tampa Times,* July 5, 1939, 5.
2. Laws of Florida, Chapter 8503, Tallahassee, Florida, 1921; "History Notes," Florida Park Service Archives, Tallahassee, Florida.
3. Nisbet, Newton A., ed. "Early History of Florida and of Sumter County." *Collection of The George Nichols Public Library,* Wildwood, Florida, 1969; "Bushnell Army Airfield Proposed Plan Public Meeting and Comment Period." *Sumter County Times,* June 20, 2013; Freeman, Paul. "Abandoned and Little-Known Airfields: Florida. Rev. 2014, website: http://www.airfields-freeman.com/FL/Airfields_FL_TampaN.htm#bushnell; Johnston, Harold. "A Bridge Not Attacked: Chemical Warfare Civilian Research During World War II." World Scientific Publishing Company, River Edge, New Jersey, 2003, p. 128; "Document Detail for IRISNUM=00156990." (http://airforcehistoryindex.org/data/000/156/990.xml). Air Force History Index.org.

Endnotes

September 13, 1988; Oliver, Mike. "Army chemicals, Fuels Haunt Sumter Site." *Orlando Sentinel.* Orlando, Florida, May 30, 1988, p. Local/State B1; Marsha Perkins, conversation with author, Bushnell, Florida, November 22, 2022; Carr, Madeline H. "Bushnell During World War II." Research paper, 2013; Archival Records, Dade Battlefield Historic State Park; Steele, Patricia. "Community Treasure." *The Villages Daily Sun,* The Villages, Florida, April 13, 2011, C4;

4. Carr, Op. cit.
5. Hagan, Thomas W. "Capital Currents." *The Miami News*, October 5, 1945, 12; "Truman Signs Allowing Sale Of Mullet Key." *Tampa Tribune,* June 19, 1948; "Dade Park Directors Renamed By Caldwell." *Miami Herald,* March 30, 1946, 2; "Management Criteria Statement, Dade Battlefield State Historic Site." Florida Department of Natural Resources, Division of Recreation and Parks, May, 1984, 9; Marsha Perkins, interview by author, Bushnell, Florida, October 2, 2013; Marsha Perkins, conversation with author, Bushnell, Florida, November 22, 2022; Pat Hardesty E-mail to Marsha Perkins, October 3, 2013.
6. "Management Criteria," Op.cit.; "Bill Asks $75,000 For Dade Memorial Park in Sumter." *Tampa Tribune,* April 15, 1953, 10; DBpedia website: https://dbpedia.org/page/J. C. Getzen Jr., accessed June 16, 2022; Journal of The Florida Senate: May 29, 1953, 934, May 31, 1955, 1686, June 1, 1961, 2105; Invitation to Bid, One Frame Residence. Florida Park Service, October 22, 1958; "City of Bushnell Home of Dade Memorial Park." *Sumter County Times,* Bushnell, Florida, February 23, 1956.
7. "Arthur Clark, Veteran Dade Battlefield Memorial Park Supervisor, Retires." *Tampa Tribune,* August 11, 1961, 14; "Dade Museum Is Dedicated." *Orlando Sentinel Times,* July 5, 1957, 3.
8. Dodrill, Jon. Position paper on the soldier statue at Dade Battlefield State Historic Site, Dade Battlefield Historic State Park archives, Bushnell, Florida, September, 1985; Frank Laumer to Lt. Wayne Edwards, October 25, 1985. Seminole Wars Foundation Laumer Library Collection.
9. "Geology and Hydrology, Including Surface Water." Dade Battlefield Historic State Park Unit Management Plan. Florida Department of Environmental Protection, October, 2017; Sumter County Florida Resolution: Opposing Efforts by The State of Florida to Change Admission to Dade Battlefield Memorial Park. Resolved May 20, 1986; Montgomery, Jeff. "Dade Park fee increase will help." *Sumter County Times,* May 30, 1991, 4.
10. Laumer, 43, Op.cit; Beremand, Dale. "What Happened to Dade's Cannon?". *Fort Armstrong Gazette,* Dade Battlefield Society, Bushnell, Florida, Summer 2012, 2; Laumer, Frank. "Massacre!". University

Press of Florida, Gainesville, Florida, 1968, 164; Smith, Wes. "Quest for Seminole War Cannon haunts expert." *Orlando Sentinel,* December 13, 2007, A1, A16.
11. "Modern Day Fence Fight Under Way At Dade Battlefield." *Tampa Tribune,* October 2, 1979, 14; Tunstall, Wes. "Proposed Dade Battlefield Road Prompts Controversy in Sumter." *Tampa Tribune,* November 12, 1979, Email from Jean McNary to the author, Dade City, Florida, June 21, 2022; 25; Letter from Jean Myers to the Heritage Conservation and Recreation Service, September 30, 1979; Letter from Ronald M. Greenberg to Jean Myers, December 13, 1979.
12. Simmons, Ernest B. "Historical Errors?" *Tampa Times,* July 7, 1938, 4; Obituary of Ernest Simmons, *Tampa Tribune,* September 28, 1952, 46.
13. Geissler, Hazel. "Bushnell Park Site Changes." *St. Petersburg Evening Independent,* November 4, 1975; Ballard, L.M. "Dade Battlefield Memorial Park In For Facelifting." *Tampa Tribune,* August 4, 1975, 15; Hencke, Tom. "Dade Battlefield Park To Get Face-Lifting." *Orlando Sentinel,* August 5, 1975, 22; "DNR Explains Proposed Changes." *Sumter County Times,* September 11, 1975, 11.
14. Ballard, Op.cit.; Harris, Kathryn. "The battle is over but a fight goes on." *St. Petersburg Times,* November 30, 1975, 109, 114; Kimball, Christopher. "Dade Battlefield: The Second Dade Massacre in 1976." Website: seminolewar.livejournal.com/141261.html, September 26, 2010; Morgan, Philip. "Sumter Countians Ambush State On Bicentennial Trail." *Tampa Tribune,* February 15, 1976, 9.
15. "Old Soldier Stands Guard At Museum." *Orlando Sentinel,* July 7, 1957, 1.
16. Washington, Ray. "A Battle Stirs Behind Dade Statue." *Gainesville Sun,* September 12, 1983, 5A, 7A; Dehart, Jason. "Hat hassles some spectators at the Dade Battlefield site." *Sumter County Times, Bushnell,* April 18, 1991, 3A; Orlando, Steve. Furor rages over battlefield statue from wrong war." *Tampa Tribune, Florida/Metro Section,* April 30, 1991. 4.
17. Bond, Bill. "Critics stew over statue in park that bears no relation to Dade." *Orlando Sentinel,* February 9, 1986, 8; Captain Lawyn C. Edwards I a letter to Dade Battlefield Memorial Park, February 2, 1981; Dehart, Op. cit.; Lebenson, Beth I. "Statue sparks battle." *Daily Commercial,* Leesburg, Florida, April 26, 1991, A1, A9; Irene S. Miller in a letter to James A. Cook, October 1, 1981; Bond, Op. cit.; Powers, Ormund. "Unusual interest from a local judge kept Dade Battlefield park alive." *Orlando Sentinel,* June 1, 1994, 4; Elizabeth K. Ehrbar in an interoffice memorandum to Jim Stevenson, August 27, 1986; "Statue's cap sparks clash at Seminole War battlefield." *Citrus County Chronicle,* April 21, 1991, 5A; Dodrill, Op.cit.; Jon W. Dodrill in a

Endnotes

letter to Frank Laumer, September 27, 1983; Jean McNary, conversation with author, Dade City, Florida, June 22, 2015.

Chapter 5: The Harmonious Expansion

1. Dale, Dick. "Dade's Death March Recalled As Ft. King Trail Is Covered Again." *Sunday Star-Banner,* Ocala, Florida, December 29, 1963; Goza, William M. "The Fort King Road 1963." Privately published booklet, 1963.
2. Memorandum from John Hale to Roy M. Brooks, Assistant Director of The Florida Park Service, May 5, 1964; Davis, Paul. "Dade Massacre Re-Lived." *St. Petersburg Independent,* September 25, 1964, 2-A; Rodriguez, Nelson and Eric Eyles. "Dade Battlefield: An Archaeological Proposal for a First Phase Investigation." *Student project for ANG 6197, Cultural Resource Management,* University of South Florida, Fall 2001, 24, 25; Sam Coverston, interview by author, Bushnell, Florida, October 10, 2014.
3. Proclamation of the Sumter County Commission, 1966; Program for Pioneer Day, Dade Memorial Park, December 28, 1966.
4. Plaque at the entrance of the museum of Dade Battlefield Historic State Park, August, 2017.
5. Laumer, Frank. Retirement Address to the Troops, January 8, 2017.
6. Letter from Jon W. Dodrill, District 5 Biologist for the State of Florida, Department of Natural Resources, to Frank Laumer, November 26, 1980; Cohen, Miriam."Tale of 1835 ambush is retold at Dade Battlefield." *St. Petersburg Times Pasco Edition,* New Port Richey, Florida, December 30, 1980, 1, 3.
7. Dodrill, Jon. "Detailed Outline of Event for Dade Battlefield Day." Open letter of lists, December 27, 1981.
8. Letter from Jon W. Dodrill, District 5 Biologist for the State of Florida, Department of Natural Resources, to Dr. John Mahon, President of the Florida Historical Society, February 1, 1982.
9. Dodrill, Jon. "Memorandum to all Dade Battlefield Commemorative Day Participants." November 22, 1982.
10. Marsha Woodard Perkins, multiple interviews by author, Bushnell, Florida, October 2 & 23, 2013, and March 11, 2021.
11. Laumer, Frank. Personal files accessed by author from October 1, 2012 to July 25, 2015; "Battle waged ages ago to rage again." *Orlando Sentinel,"* December 25, 1985; "Dade Massacre re-enacted." *St. Petersburg Times,"* December 23, 1985; Campbell, Ramsey. "It's war as Seminole meet soldiers in staging of massacre." *Orlando Sentinel,* December 29, 1985; "300 re-enact Dade Massacre." *Orlando Sentinel,* January 2, 1986, 8.
12. Virginia Bell, interview by author, Bushnell, Florida, January 9, 2018; Marsha Woodard Perkins, interview by author, Bushnell, Florida,

March 11, 2021; "Old Fashioned $uccess." *Fort Armstrong Gazette, Newsletter of Dade Battlefield Society,* December 1987; Bell, Virginia S. Dade Battlefield Society, Inc. Open memorandum to the public, November, 1988.
13. Laumer, Frank. Personal files …, Op.cit.
14. Personal observations by author, Bushnell, Florida, from January 3 to March 8, 2015; Laumer, Op. cit.
15. Clifton, Larry. "Dade Battlefield Park could be history." *Sumter County Times,* Bushnell, Florida, January 20, 2011; Powers, A.D. "The DADE MASSACRE and Dade Memorial Park." Privately published booklet, St. Petersburg, Florida, 16; Personal observations by author, Bushnell, Florida, from January 1, 2009 to July 22, 2015; Locklear, Brenda. "Byway to benefit businesses/community." *Sumter County Times,* Bushnell, Florida, February 6, 2014.
16. Reichman, Bob. "Dade Battlefield Park: A push to spark attendance." *Sumter County Times,* Bushnell, Florida, June 16, 2011; Memorandum from Brian Fugate to Interested Parties, "2021-22 Economic Impact Assessment Report, Florida State Park System." Florida Department of Environmental Protection, September 26, 2022; Website of Dade Battlefield Society, dadebattlefield.com, accessed on August 26, 2022; Steele, Martin. "Celebrating the 4th, a day early." *Sumter County Times,* Bushnell, Florida, July 9, 2015.

Appendix A
1. Adams, Jamie. "March remembers bygone days at Dade Park." *Sumter County Times.* Bushnell, Florida. February 18, 1999.
2. Interviews of Marsha Perkins by author, Bushnell Florida, October 2, 2013, October 23, 2013, and March 11, 2021; Glidewell, Jan. "March that made a match." *St. Petersburg Times,* December 22, 1989; Conversation between Marsha Perkins and the author, Bushnell, Florida, November 22, 2022.
3. Interview of John W. Outlaw, Sr. by author, Inverness, Florida, October 5, 2013; Interview of Frank Hamilton by author, Bushnell, Florida, October 15, 2013; Interview of Josephine Strong-Simmons by author, Bushnell, Florida, May 25, 2017; Interview of Martin Steele by author, Bushnell, Florida, February 17, 2015; Interview of Ginger Bell Realmuto by author, Bushnell, Florida, January 9, 2018.
4. Interview of Gayle Hunt by author, Bushnell, Florida, November 4, 2014; League, Susan L. "Gayle Hunt: An Unsung Hero of Sumter County." *Sumter News-Sun,* November 10, 2021; Arne, Sigrid. "Public Enemies---G-Man Hoover Names First Eight on New 1938 List." *Reading Eagle,* Reading, Pennsylvania, January 30, 1938; Interview of Scrammy Hunt by author, Bushnell, Florida, 2018.

Endnotes

5. Interview of Sam Coverston by author, Bushnell, Florida, October 10, 2014; Savage, Carole. "School set for Coverston remembrance." *Sumter County Times,* March 9, 2017, A1; Interview of Marsha Perkins by author, Bushnell, Florida, November 1, 2022.

About the Author

Steven Rinck served eight years as president of the Seminole Wars Foundation, and still maintains active roles with that not-for-profit group. An avid student of history for all of his life, the retired Pasco County teacher and principal is past president of the Dade Battlefield Society, a trustee of the Fort King Heritage Foundation and a member of the Florida Historical Society. He is also active with historical societies in Sumter, Hernando, and Pasco counties. Steven is a consultant for the Pioneer Florida Museum & Village and a proud supporter of the Seminole Tribe's Ah-Tah-Thi-Ki Museum. He reenacts at Second Seminole War, Civil War, and World War II events, and enjoys performing first-person historical impressions for school, military and civic groups.

Beyond the Battle is Steven's first published literary endeavor, and he is excited that the personal stories of sacrifice and perseverance that were made in order to bring proper recognition to Dade Battlefield are at last being told.

The Author photographing Judge Koonce at the 1914 Sumter County Courtroom.

Courtesy Bill Gruber